KT-464-500

True Stories of Shipwreck, Piracy and Buried Treasure

Rosemary Kingsland

Line drawings by

Mary French and Gareth Floyd

ANGUS & ROBERTSON · PUBLISHERS

ANGUS & ROBERTSON · PUBLISHERS
London · Sydney · Melbourne · Singapore · Manila



First published in Great Britain 1980 by Angus & Robertson (UK) Ltd
10 Earlham Street, London WC2H 9LP



ISBN 0 207 95876 9

Typeset by BSC Graphics Ltd, London
Printed and bound in Great Britain by
R. J. Acford, Industrial Estate, Chichester, Sussex

# Contents

# *Introduction*

Men with treasure, real treasure—bars of gold and cascades of silver, flashing diamonds, rich rubies and emeralds, huge pearls, paintings and art treasures, secret documents—to hide have one thing in common: they invariably concealed it on an island, as adventurers and pirates have always done.

Islands are special places. Today, with air transport, the world is a very small place in terms of travel and communication. The last wild frontiers are falling all the time. Darkest Africa, Arabia, even South America, have lost their mystery; today we can go fairly easily anywhere in the world. But islands remain difficult to reach, especially small ones. Some are still remote, mysterious places in tossing seas and often untouched by civilization. And in the days before aeroplanes and when sailing-ships were still primitive, they must have been even more unapproachable. Small wonder, then, that it was to these remote, difficult to reach islands that those with treasure to hide sailed, there to conceal their treasure to keep it safe.

All the islands described in this book can be found in a good atlas. They range from Caldy, off the coast of Wales, where the great riches of an abbey were hidden from King Henry VIII in 1534, to La Plata, off the coast of South America, where Drake concealed tons of silver captured from the Spanish in 1577; from Taumatos, remote in the Pacific, where millions of pounds' worth of gold and jewels were concealed in a sea-pool in 1859, to Elba, where treasure and top-secret documents stolen by the Nazis during the Second World War were taken before the fall of Italy. The sixteen islands described are in Europe, North and South America, Australia—from the Pacific to the Atlantic. Wherever you are there is an island that possibly one day you could journey to in search of booty that would make you rich beyond your wildest dreams!

The treasures described here were almost always associated with pirates to whom treachery and murder were a way of life in the days when sailing-ships roamed the world. Pirates themselves were cut-throat robbers who had no loyalty to any king or country, and who swooped on any ship of every nation, including their own. There was also another sort of pirate, a privateer. He was a kind of commissioned pirate, actually given permission by his own country to rob his enemies; but if he ever stole from his own country's ships, then he was a called a pirate and hunted down and hanged. The treasure stolen by privateers was shared with the king. Other treasures described were hidden in times of war, revolution or even just by accident.

The most exciting thing of all about buried treasure, of course, is the fact that all of it actually exists—if only its hiding-place could be discovered. These are true stories of what the treasure is, how it was stolen and from whom, how it was hidden and by whom—and where it is.

Why, then, has it not been found? The answer in each case is simple. It has not been found because it was hidden on some of the most remote places in the world—places so remote that the journeys to them in most cases are far beyond the reach of the average person. And, even more important, it takes a mind as cunning and astute as the person's who buried it to be able to follow the clues that will lead to its hiding-place. But attempts have been made to find the treasure hidden on these islands. Mutineers, buccaneers, pirates, and even respectable adventurers and treasure-searchers have all tried to find the treasure. They were in search of riches and an easy life which, however, they never found. Some, satiated with blood and destruction, died of starvation, murder or exposure within inches of the treasure they sought. Others gave up in despair after a lifetime of searching. Who knows which fortunate person may be the one lucky enough to find it?

# 1. La Plata

*Ecuador, Pacific Ocean*

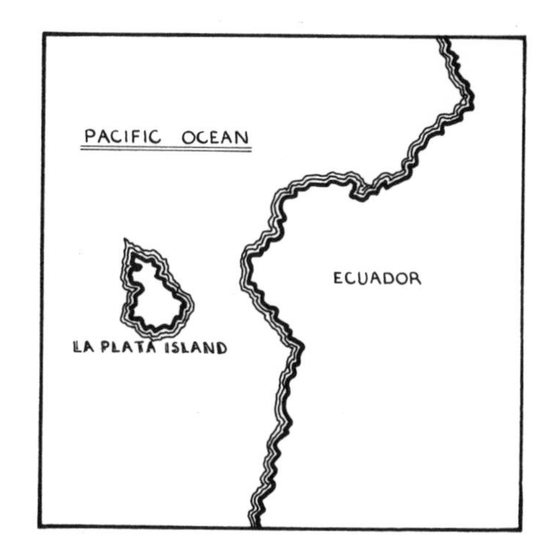


Robert Louis Stevenson opens *Treasure Island* with the words: 'Squire Trelawney, Dr Livesey, and the rest of these gentlemen having asked me to write down the whole particulars about Treasure Island, from the beginning to the end, keeping nothing back but the bearings of the island, and that only because there is still treasure not yet lifted, I take up my pen. . . .'

The island on which Stevenson based his book was La Plata, off the coast of Ecuador, South America, and the reason why he kept nothing back but the bearings of the island (apart from its real name) was because there *was* treasure there, which he himself went off to seek. So far as is known he did not find any, but just under fifty years later in 1930, someone else did, which proves that Stevenson was simply unlucky.

La Plata means 'silver' and it really is an island of silver—buried silver from Sir Francis Drake's own ship, the *Golden Hind*.

Sir Francis Drake sailed from Plymouth in November 1577 with orders from Queen Elizabeth I to break Spain's jealously guarded and rich dominions in the South Seas, as the Pacific was then known. He created havoc along the coast of South America, plundering the cities and looting them of their wealth. After a successful raid on the main port in Peru he learned from a prisoner that the Spanish royal treasure-ship, *La Nuestra de la Conception*—Drake nicknamed her *Cacafuego,* or spitfire—laden with gold and silver, had sailed for Panama a few days earlier.

Compared with the Spanish galleon the *Golden Hind* was fast and light, and it easily overtook the Spaniards. After a long sea-battle that ended with the Spanish ship drifting helplessly in the water Drake took possession of the treasure aboard. There were fourteen chests full of silver coins, twenty-six tons of silver ingots, eighty chests of gold, and large quantities of pearls, gold chains and jewels.

Drake realized that with all this additional weight the *Golden Hind* would sink in the first storm they ran into and that he must lighten the load. La Plata happened to be the nearest land, so he dropped anchor in a sheltered bay where a certain amount of the prize-money was divided among the crew, and the many tons of the remainder jettisoned overboard in fifty feet of water, its bearings carefully, and secretly, recorded. Drake planned to return to the island at a later date, but for the next twenty years he was so busy sailing around the world, commanding fleets of ships in open war with Spain, sacking and looting their cities in the West Indies, and helping to defeat the Spanish Armada that he was never able to get back to La Plata.

Then in 1596 when in command of a naval force fighting the Spanish, he was killed, and it was several centuries before his treasure was eventually discovered.

A hundred years after Drake's successful ventures into the South Seas more treasure was hidden on La Plata by the buccaneers who were roaming the Caribbean. They crossed the isthmus of Panama to the Pacific in search of larger prizes, as the Caribbean was overcrowded with fortune-hunters and profits were higher on the west coast. Five buccaneers teamed up, one of whom, Richard Sawkins, according even to his enemies was 'the bravest and most respected of all'. They captured five Spanish ships and sailed south with them to La Plata where they divided the treasure and buried most of it on the island.

The island, conveniently located close to the mainland and well stocked with provisions in the form of wildlife, soon became the haunt of so many pirates that the Spanish viceroy of Peru had all the goats on the island shot and the trees cut down to discourage pirates from operating in that area by making the island barren.

Because of that, Captain Stradling of the privateer *Cinque Ports* very nearly ended his days on La Plata and his treasure too certainly did. The *Cinque Ports* had captured an enormously rich Spanish treasure-ship and, laden down with gold and silver, they ran into a storm. When Captain

Stradling saw that the ship was not going to survive in the storm he unloaded the treasure into longboats and made for La Plata. During a terrible voyage of over a thousand miles scurvy, injuries and lack of provisions wiped out most of the crew, but Stradling eventually arrived at La Plata where he hid the treasure in a cliff cave, afterwards blasting the entrance to conceal it. The men lived on the island, managing as best they could with little food; they had no powder for their muskets so they could shoot nothing for food. By the time a Spanish ship arrived there were only four survivors; they were taken to the mainland and made to work as slaves in the Peruvian mines. Three of them died because of harsh treatment, but the fourth, Captain Stradling, was eventually sent to Spain where he was captured by the French, who sent him to England in exchange for French prisoners-of-war held by the British.

In due course, after recovering his strength and raising funds, Stradling set sail in a small frigate for La Plata to collect his treasure. But the frigate was wrecked in a storm off the coast of Newfoundland with the loss of all on board, and the treasure of the *Cinque Ports* to this day remains still hidden in its secret cave on the island of La Plata.

Few attempts have been made to locate the treasure—that of Drake, the buccaneers and Stradling—either buried on the island or lying in the sea in shallow water. In 1930 the dredger *Goole* recovered ten tons of silver bars (it's not known what happened to them), but the captain reported that the greater part of the treasure was buried deep in the soft sand, and that dredging attempts were only driving it deeper into the sea-bed.

There is still a great amount of treasure offshore, and there are also substantial caches on the island itself; it only remains for a well-organized expedition to locate and unearth it—and make all its members incredibly rich.

# 2. Elba

*Italy, Mediterranean Sea*

During the Second World War (1939-45) Mussolini used his power as dictator of Italy to collect together a vast personal fortune. It included four tons of gold from the Italian state bank, jewels stripped from wealthy families, the enormously heavy crown of Ethiopia, paintings and art treasures, and wooden crates stuffed with stolen and forged currency. When the Allies invaded Italy Mussolini headed for Milan (en route to Germany if the worst came to the worst) and there he met his death at the hands of the partisans, who left him hanging upside-down from a lamp-post.

His treasure followed him—but it never reached Milan. It vanished somewhere along the coast-roads, and although the sixteen men guarding it were tried and convicted of complicity nothing has been seen or heard of it since.

Italy, during the final days before the Allied invasion, was in a state of turmoil, torn not only by the invading troops from the exterior but also by the mixed loyalties of the Italians themselves. Some were fascist, others communist; there were partisans who fought as Italians against the Germans, and there were those who fought for the Germans—and there were those who were traitors to everyone, concerned only for their own skins. There were also the retreating Germans, surrounded by their enemies, the Allies.

When the Mussolini treasure vanished it went into this maelstrom of confusion and so it is hardly surprising that on the face of it no one knows very much about it. Even the sheer quantity of treasure—the six trucks used to carry it—would not have been remarked upon then when arms and ammunition were being transported, when trucks were full of troops, when partisans hijacked the Germans and when whole villages were on the move for fear of reprisal. However, there *are* those who even today know something, and it is by piecing together their fragmented stories that the route taken by this treasure can be followed.

Most people believe that the treasure was driven into the Italian Alps in the north and hidden there, or perhaps taken from the point where it disappeared to Tuscany—to Carrara, where Michelangelo quarried the marble for his famous statues and where there are huge caves and caverns. But all this is surmise.

The actual place where the treasure was taken, according to local stories, was to a large estate once owned by Napoleon's sister, Princess Pauline Borghese, in the hills above the town of Pisa in northern Italy. This villa was taken over during the War by the German SS. Even today there is a lasting feud between some families: between those who joined the Germans and those who were partisans.

The hill on which the villa stands is riddled with caves, and some of the local men declare—not to strangers—that it was here that the treasure was taken, up the secretive forest-covered hill, to be concealed in the caves and guarded by the SS.

The villa is a stone's throw from the ports of Pisa and Viareggio, and it was to one of these ports that the treasure was taken later when the fall of Italy looked imminent. People in the know say that a sea-journey was safer than any road, as the roads were filled with the mass exodus of the German and Italian armies from the south before the waves of the Allied forces. They say that the officers of the SS and some local farmers who were employed by them loaded the treasure on a boat and headed south fifty miles to the island

of Elba. With their authority as members of the feared SS there was no problem in requisitioning a boat. No questions were asked and the cargo was not even examined.

Elba is riddled with caves in its limestone eastern coast—and with iron mines, where the ore had been dug out from the ground for over two thousand years. It was to one of the lonely beaches on the east coast that the treasure was taken and concealed in the cliffs.

Nothing is known about what happened to the Italians used in this work, but almost certainly they were killed at once to keep the whereabouts of the treasure secret. The SS officers could not risk them returning to their homes and describing their night's activities; obviously they themselves would want to return later, even if it took years, and have the treasure safe for themselves.

But the boat used, the *David,* it is recorded, was sunk on its return journey with the loss of all on board, and the secret of the hiding-place of the Mussolini millions and of the fabulous crown of Ethiopia was lost.

All that is known is that somewhere on Elba the treasure is hidden and the only men who knew for sure where it was concealed were drowned in the Mediterranean.

# 3. Auckland Islands

*New Zealand, South Pacific Ocean*

It must be rare indeed for a ship carrying gold to sink inside a huge cave in the cliffs of an island, and for that treasure never to have been recovered. But that is exactly what appears to have happened in the case of *General Grant* which sank in the cliffs off Auckland Island, three hundred and fifty miles south of New Zealand—and not connected to the New Zealand city of Auckland.

The cave into which the *General Grant* was swept by strong currents was enormous. The ship was a fine three-masted schooner of twelve hundred tons. Her official cargo was largely wool and some gold; her *unofficial* cargo was also gold, since many of her passengers were returning home to England via South America having struck it rich in the Australian gold-fields. The exact value of the gold bullion can only be guessed at; those were the times when men said little about their wealth, although a fairly accurate estimate then put the value at two million pounds—worth about fifty million pounds today.

The ship sailed from Melbourne on 4 May 1866 and, for the superstitious, nine days later, the 13 May, really was an unlucky day for those aboard as they approached the Auckland Islands. The night was dark and misty but there was a light wind—not the usual conditions for a shipwreck. The captain had set his course for the channel between the main island in the Auckland group and the small rocky Disappointment Island when the wind suddenly dropped and the ship swung at the mercy of the powerful currents. The crew worked frantically, but with the sails empty of wind there was nothing they could do and the sea was too deep to drop anchor. In the darkness the ship was swept remorselessly towards the towering cliffs of Auckland Island, and at about 11.30 p.m. it struck the Beehive Rocks. The rudder was smashed so all control of the ship was lost.

For the already terrified passengers it must have seemed that they were entering the jaws of hell when the tall ship began to be swallowed up by a huge enveloping cave in the cliff side. With the roar of the surf booming and re-echoing through the cavern it must have seemed that their final moments had come. But the captain was strangely calm and reassuring. He saw that although they were trapped in the mouth of the cave they were in no immediate danger of sinking, so he decided to wait until dawn before taking further action.

At dawn he sent out two boats, one of which was loaded with sufficient tackle to haul the other boat clear, if necessary. Unfortunately, however, the Captain had not reckoned on the action of the tide as it fell. As the level of the sea dropped, it released the main mast which had been jammed against the top of the cave, and with the ebb and flow of the water, the ship was sucked further inside the cave. As the main mast again scraped against the lowering roof of the cave, showers of rock fell on the terrified passengers. Finally, the main mast jammed in a cleft in the roof and was held fast, but with the see-saw action of the sea the hull of the ship began to split apart. The sea poured in as the deck planks parted. Some passengers dived overboard hoping to reach the two boats already launched, but few survived in the rough seas and strong currents. About forty others sat in the longboat on deck waiting for the ship to

sink beneath them so that they could float off, as there was insufficient room in the cave to lower the boat over the side in the normal way. But the waves quickly swamped them, the boat capsized, and only three people managed to swim to the safety of the two boats outside the cavern.

With the exception of the small amount of gold the passengers carried with them, all the bullion went down with the ship. Fourteen men and one woman survived to sit cold and wet in the two boats outside the mouth of the cavern. For a while they waited in the hope that some of the sixty-eight remaining passengers, including women and children, would appear, but when none did the survivors rejected the idea of scaling the overhanging cliffs as being more dangerous than staying in the boats, and they made for Disappointment Island which had often been used by whalers and sealers and had a reasonable landing-beach.

Although it was May, the Aucklands were bleak, swept by icy winds and rain, and the already frozen castaways had little to warm them. They had some tins of soup and one match—the rest were spoilt—with which they managed to light a fire that they had to keep going night and day. They caught seals and roasted the meat, and with the skins made rough but serviceable clothes. They discovered an old hut used by former whalers. This was practically in ruins but they used seal-skins to patch it up as a shelter from the biting winds.

The *General Grant* had gone down on 14 May 1866. On 21 November 1867, an astonishing eighteen months after the tragedy, a whaler saw their signal fire, and the starving and bitterly cold survivors were rescued. They arrived in New Zealand in January 1868.

The gold that had gone down with the *General Grant* interested many people, and various salvage parties were formed. The first one set out with James Teer, one of the survivors of the wreck, and it managed to locate the cave. Bad weather prevented the party from entering at once, and while they were heaved to a violent quarrel broke out and unaccountably, having come so far and getting so close, the attempt was abandoned.

The next attempt in 1870 was more tragic. The schooner *Daphne* landed at Port Ross on the main island and the captain left her in charge of the cook and a boy while he set off with the remaining five members of the crew in a whale-boat to locate the cave. They sailed round the north-west cape and completely vanished. Eventually the cook and the boy took the ship's dinghy and tried to find the missing crew but, apart from an oar and part of a boat washed up on the shore, they found nothing.

Seven years later in 1877 Cornelius Drew, another survivor of the *General Grant,* found the cave but could not enter it because of heavy seas. On his return to New Zealand he said that he had seen a dark shape which could have been the wreck of the *General Grant* lying just outside the entrance to the cave, on the south side, indicating that currents were shifting the wreck out of the cave into deeper water.

This information probably put many men off further searches since it wasn't until 1911 that a Captain Sorensen, an American, formed a syndicate to recover the gold. He had a novel idea and one that attracted wide publicity. The other treasure-hunters, he said, had gone about it wrongly. They should never have attempted to approach the cavern from the sea. The tides and weather were never right in that part of the world, he declared. His plan was to build a road across the island from the east to a position directly above the cave and then erect a cantilevered platform projecting twenty-five feet out from the cliff. From that, two cables could be lowered and anchored in the sea. An elevator would be suspended from these cables and then, regardless of weather, a diver could be raised and lowered into the sea.

The idea was certainly original. The Sorensen Salvage Company was formed and a steamer purchased. Orders were placed in England for heavy lifting machinery, and the whole operation rather grandly set in motion with a great deal of publicity. But it fell very flat when, with a large crowd waiting on the quay to see them off, a writ was issued preventing them from leaving port because of a four hundred pounds repair bill which had not been paid.

The American Deep-Sea Exploring Company was the next to be formed to look for the gold, but their ship sank even before leaving American waters.

Then in 1915 a Captain Catling made two attempts for the gold. The weather beat him on his first attempt, but eventually he made several dives both inside and outside the cave. There was no sign of the wreck outside the cave and only a few planks of wood on the rocky bed of the cave inside. It seemed that the *General Grant* had been pounded to pieces, plank by plank, and swept out to sea. There was no sign of the gold. One conclusion Catling reached, probably to save his face at his lack of success, was that the captain of the *Daphne* had located the wreck, taken the gold, and had then sunk on the way back, but this seems a very unlikely theory.

This was not the end of the story. Treasure-hunters have one thing in common: they are insatiable optimists. Some of them contended that Catling had searched the wrong cave. Perhaps they were right; there are many other large caves along those rocky cliffs not yet explored.

In 1934 an Australian, Mr Sheehy, embarked on what was to be the most careful research into the treasure, and he devoted many years to it, writing over a thousand letters attempting to establish the rightful owners of the gold in anticipation of salvaging it, but in 1952, because of bad health, he sold his rights and information to Bill Havens, another Australian. Among the papers were some notes written by William Sanguilly, one of the *General Grant* survivors who had been in charge of the cargo manifests. He stated that acting under Captain Loughlin's orders he had documented some of the gold cargo as spelter (impure zinc) to deceive the pirates who were thought to be on the ship itself disguised as passengers.

Bill Havens was no luckier than all his ill-fated predecessors in his search. His ship, the *Absit Omen* ('let no evil befall'), was wrecked on its way to New Zealand on 31 December 1959.

That appears to be the end of the story to date. In September 1962 the New Zealand Marine Department announced that no further salvage applications would be considered. They feel that conditions in the Auckland Islands are too dangerous and that it is their duty to save reckless treasure-hunters from the run of bad luck and disaster that seems to be dogging the lost gold of the *General Grant*.

# 4. Tortuga

*Haiti, Caribbean Sea*

The hump-backed island of Tortuga in the West Indies is an Aladdin's cave for seekers of buried and sunken treasure. The island is ringed by sixteenth- and seventeenth-century Spanish wrecks containing, as one historian put it, 'as yet unrecovered millions in gold, silver and jewels'. On the island itself in secret caves and buried deep in the forests are the fortunes of pirates long since dead.

Tortuga appears, like a monster sea-turtle in shape, riding upon the waves about an hour's journey from the Haiti coast in the Caribbean. It was first seen by Christopher Columbus in 1494; he named it Tortuga—the turtle—after its shape. The island is so thickly wooded that even today, after centuries of occupation, first by the Spanish and then by the French, very little of the interior has been explored. Its beautiful trees range from lofty cedars, coconuts and mangoes to oranges, lemons, bananas, figs and aromatic spices. Cattle and pigs were taken to the island by the first Spanish settlers who, in a bout of Christian fervour, slaughtered the pagan Indian population before leaving to cross over to the mainland of South America, attracted by the gold of the Aztecs and Incas, the native peoples of Mexico and Peru. They were not able to take their animals with them and the beasts were abandoned, growing wild as they roamed free and multiplying with amazing rapidity.

The French settled on the island in around 1530. They tilled the earth, Indian-fashion, with sticks hardened by fire, and planted yams, manioc and tobacco, as well as simple domestic vegetables, and these, together with a great variety of fish, turtles and crabs that could be caught by hand to roast over fires, game birds, wild boar and numerous other animals that produced fresh meat, must have made Tortuga seem like a paradise—as it still is today.

It was an island that was fairly easy to protect. It is twenty-two miles long and some four miles wide. Its southern side looks towards Haiti and on that side has a deep safe anchorage protected by the high rocks and outjutting reefs at the entrance. The rocky north side of the island is so uninviting and dangerous that it was called the 'iron coast'.

Word of the island's delights soon spread and seamen came: deserters, shipwrecked sailors, criminals, all with one thing in common: a desire to live a free and easy life. Meat was so plentiful that they traded it, mainly to passing Dutchmen, first smoking it in strips over a wooden grill which the natives called a 'boucan'. From the word boucan to buccaneer was an easy enough step, but from being hunters of beasts in the forest to becoming hunters of sailors on the high seas was a much slower process. It was a long time before the word "buccaneer" struck terror into the hearts of all merchant seamen.

The basis of that terror was the exceptional loyalty these first buccaneers had for each other. In the first place there were no women on the island to split up friendships. Indeed, their slogan was 'we need no women'. The men could think in the wide terms of freedom and not within the narrower limits of home and children. With loyal friends at their backs they became more audacious, knowing that each would support the other. They usually hunted in pairs, known as matelots, and the young men who accompanied them as musket-loaders and servants were called valets.

These buccaneers were a mixed bunch of French, English and Dutch and they all hated the Spanish. To them, the Conquistadores stood for all that was vile and therefore fair

game in their search for plunder.

At first they took to sea in nothing more than home-made canoes, rowing along the coast at night until they surprised and overcame the crew of some small schooner. Later, as their ranks swelled and they boarded and captured merchant-ships, the crew of the merchantman were invited to join the pirates. Some would do so willingly, others only under compulsion. Any member of the crew who resisted would be killed and his body thrown overboard. Large quantities of gold and silver which the Spaniards had looted from the Incas and were taking home to Spain were captured and hidden away in secret places on Tortuga. Also captured were stocks of flour, linen, and other stores intended for Spanish garrisons in South America.

As they grew in strength and captured larger and faster vessels, the buccaneers pillaged the coastal towns of Santa Domingo (now the Dominican and Haiti republics). Houses and churches were stripped of their treasures, and important citizens taken for ransom. Nearly all this vast wealth found its way to Tortuga, but not all—the buccaneers were surprisingly pious men in their fashion and booty taken from one church would sometimes be donated to another. One captain even held mass on his ship after a successful raid and captured a priest to conduct it.

But by now for most of the buccaneers the rule was 'plunder, and home to Tortuga for the good life', and in a period when piracy was at its peak the island became a regular pirate republic and an important retreat for British sailors during a period of successful Spanish raids on Haiti, then owned by England. It was thought expedient by the English navy to establish a storehouse that could be made safe from attack, and such a stronghold was built in 1630, but in 1641 the Spanish attacked Tortuga, defeated the British garrison, and massacred every settler found.

Those who escaped returned later and gathered new recruits from every European trading nation. For three-quarters of a century they were the scourge of Spanish-American trade, and particularly of Spanish treasure-ships. In 1663, a British frigate, *The Oxford,* was sent to Jamaica by Charles II on a privateering mission and it captured a great deal of Spanish treasure in the name of the king, but the men concealed a large part of it on the island for their own use, and as far as is known none of this treasure has ever been recovered.

The island was eventually taken over by the French who decided that women on the island would tame the buccaneers. In 1669 a shipload of young women sailed from France to become the chains that entrapped the buccaneers. It is not all that difficult to imagine the type of girls they were. According to the nuns in charge of them, they were 'debauched young girls who knew the truth about themselves'.

Family life weakened the basis of loyalty between the men which in the past had held the community together. They began to stay at home with their French wives, and the terror that had once struck into the hearts of their victims became a thing of the past. A certain amount of piracy still continued, for some men never accept hearth and home, but the fiery heart had gone out of it. As time passed, the Spaniards raided the island again and again in vain attempts to recover some of the treasure stolen from them, and within a hundred years of the arrival of the women the island was deserted and the buccaneers' dream of freedom was over.

All that remains of that dream today is the occasional cache of treasure uncovered by the present native settlers as they till the ground. A team of enthusiastic treasure-hunters with little effort could become extraordinarily rich, for legend has it that immense quantities of treasure lie not very far below the surface of that beautiful and almost deserted island.

# 5. Isles of Shoals

*New Hampshire, USA, Atlantic Ocean*

Many treasure-troves exist only in the imagination or in legend, though it is said that even legends are always based in fact, and some stories of buried treasure are based in fact itself. This is the case of the buried treasures of the Isles of Shoals, a collection of wind-swept sandbanks off the coast of New Hampshire, USA. Whose was the treasure? Did Blackbeard hide it on those dangerous sandy shoals, or did Captain John Quelch? Or both?

Blackbeard—Captain Edward Teach—'the wickedest pirate ever', is one man to whom there clings the legend of great chests of blood-drenched treasure, and some of these chests, it is said, were buried on two of the small islands that make up the Shoals group. Others say that the evidence points to the treasure being left there by John Quelch, an arrogant scoundrel if ever there was one. What there is no doubt about is that the treasure is there–untold wealth for the person lucky enough to find it.

Quelch was everything one expects a pirate to be, bloodthirsty and treacherous, a swaggering swashbuckler who ended his life on the gallows. Before he died, however, he set the authorities on a merry chase from Boston to Brazil, slaughtering the crews and passengers of nine Portuguese ships before sending them all to the bottom of the sea and making off with his plunder of everything of value from sugar and salt to bars of silver and gold.

Quelch's story began in 1703 when the British governor of Massachusetts commissioned the brigantine *Charles* as a privateer to prey upon ships flying the French flag, as England was at war with France. Privateers were private vessels commissioned to seize and plunder the enemy's ships. Should the crew of a privateer turn on its own country's ships, or on those of a neutral country, however, they were treated as pirates and hanged.

The *Charles* was commanded by Captain Plowman who fell sick just before she was due to sail, and asked the governor if he could be relieved of his command. The truth was that Captain Plowman did not like the look of his crew, and he was right in his judgment, for before he could leave the ship he was locked in his cabin and his second-in-command, Captain Quelch, took over.

As soon as they were on the high seas, Captain Plowman was murdered and his body thrown overboard. Later Quelch swore that his captain had died of his illness, but the evidence was that he was murdered, and no satisfactory explanation could be given as to why Captain Plowman had been prevented from leaving the ship.

The *Charles,* with the skull and crossbones flying from its mast, took a southerly course for the area around Jamaica and Cuba, then known as the Spanish Main, but the Main was already crowded with pirates and privateers, which meant that the pickings were lean, so Quelch continued south until he reached Brazilian waters. Here he attacked and sacked nine Portuguese ships, obtaining a rich haul, mostly of silver from the famous Brazilian mines, which set him on a direct course for the gallows.

For four months Quelch terrorized shipping bound to and from Brazil, and with holds bulging with rum, silks, flour, rice, gold, silver and jewels, he set his course back to

Massachusetts. A more audacious move on the part of a pirate is hard to find in the annals of piracy. But Quelch banked on two things: that his story of Captain Plowman's dying of sickness would be believed, and that greed on the part of the governor would overcome the governor's scruples as to the source of the treasure.

The captain and his men swaggered ashore with the air of conquering heroes, their pockets full of the gold they were itching to spend. But Quelch's luck was running out, and the drunken state of his crew, and their bragging, was helping it to run out faster.

Quelch told the governor that he had had no luck with French ships as none had been sighted, but that he had come across a shipwrecked Spanish galleon and that it was her cargo that now lay in his hold. The governor, however, recognized the difference between Spanish and Portuguese markings on the sample of gold coins Quelch had with him, and this, coupled with reports of the drunken boastings of the crew, caused the governor to have them arrested and thrown into prison.

The rest of the crew on board, alarmed at the way things were going, bribed the captain of the *Larramore Galley,* at anchor nearby, with promises of untold wealth, to turn pirate and join them. Under cover of darkness they quickly transferred the bullion and jewels from the one ship to the other. Then, with the Jolly Roger—as the pirate's flag of skull and crossbones is known—flying from the mast, the *Larramore Galley* set sail for the Isles of Shoals, a few miles off the coast in Boston bay.

The captain of the *Larramore Galley* had previously been of good character, but the treasure was rich and he was overwhelmed by greed. He was destined to have a very short career as a pirate. The dangers of having a rogue pirate-ship directly off the New England coast did not escape the notice of the English colony's authorities. They ordered that the ship should be pursued and captured and her crew brought to justice. An army officer, Major Sewall, was persuaded to take charge of an expedition, and he set sail with a crew of forty-two men in search of the pirate ship.

Major Sewall sighted the ship before he himself was seen and pretended he was a fishing boat until he could get within range. There was no watch on the *Larramore Galley,* and he soon saw why. The ship was lying at anchor off the Isles of Shoals and all the crew was busily engaged in burying the treasure in the sand. It was not until Major Sewall was almost upon the pirates that they smelt danger and made a dash to their gun positions. But the major simply ordered his forty-two men to show themselves, and this sudden display of military strength knocked any thought of fight out of the pirates. They surrendered.

The treasure they were in the process of burying was recovered, but the remainder of the treasure had already been buried in a number of places. Where those places were the pirates wouldn't say, and when they were all hanged their secret died with them. What is known is that a large part of the booty captured from nine Portuguese ships lies buried somewhere in those sands, and that a few years later, round about 1715, the gruesome burying of a further chest of treasure took place in the same area by the notorious Blackbeard, Captain Teach.

Edward Teach, or Thatch, was born in 1690 in Bristol, a city of sea-farers. He went to sea at an early age and saw Bristol no more. He enjoyed adding to his audacious and swashbuckling image and quickly became a classic, archetypal, ranting, raving pirate. It was not long before he got his famous name of Blackbeard, and from all accounts and from illustrations he presented a terrifying picture. He must have been slightly mad. He never cut his hair or beard which covered most of his face and became the talk of two continents. His hair was so long that he arranged it in dozens of devilish-looking ribbon-bedecked pigtails that stuck out from his face at all angles. With wisps of burning hemp tucked under his dashing hat, fizzing candles and firecrackers tied in his beard and hair, and several pistols

slung around his neck, most of his victims succumbed to fear and quickly surrendered. Those who were defeated were cut up into pieces by the several sabres and knives Blackbeard carried in his belt, or they were made to walk the plank to yells of crazy laughter and horrible oaths. His store of treasure soon piled up since he was a very competent pirate. There are so many legends relating to the fact that he buried most of his treasure on several of the small islands, particularly Smuttynose and Londoner, that make up the Isles of Shoals, that one is forced to accept that there must be some truth in the stories.

An astonishing truth is that this amazing villain married fourteen wives, and the fourteenth was the one selected to guard the secret of his treasure. Cynics say that it is hard to believe that a man who had so little regard for women that he could marry and discard them so readily would have entrusted the secret of his treasure to any one of them.

Mrs Teach the fourteenth remained for many years on her house on Londoner Island where her husband placed her, and when she died in 1735, seventeen years after her husband had been killed by the English in a violent battle at sea, it was said that her ghost continued to guard the treasure.

The ghost of another wife is also said to guard the treasure. This was Prudence Lutrelle, a sixteen-year-old who, unlike most young girls who would have been terrified at the sight of Blackbeard, was fascinated by his colourful clothes and dashing swagger. A wedding ceremony was performed but only a few days after the wedding Blackbeard grew tired of Prudence. He took his young bride on his ship, not as part of a honeymoon cruise, but as the first part of her journey to death. She was locked away in her cabin and no one was allowed to see her. They sailed along the coast in darkness and at Plum Point, off the Isles of Shoals, Blackbeard ordered six of his men ashore with him. In their longboat they took with them an iron-bound treasure-chest, picks and shovels—and Prudence.

Blackbeard selected the site and commanded the men to dig. When the chest was buried, he murdered Prudence and threw her on top of the treasure. A large boulder was rolled over the grave, and Blackbeard told them: 'What you have seen this night you'll forget, or I'll slit your throats—slowly!'

The story may have been a fantasy, as pirates' tales often are, but what is true is that Prudence did vanish after the voyage. Why she should have been murdered is not recorded. Was Blackbeard thinking of his tragic young wife when he once said, 'Nobody but the devil and myself know where my treasure is, and the longer-lived of the two of us shall have it'?

Bars of silver have been found on the Isles of Shoals after storms which have shifted the sand, and there was the story reported in a New England newspaper of 1950 that a treasure-hunting consortium had discovered something big in the way of gold on the Isles, and they had made arrangements for a local bank to stay open to receive it. What happened then was not told; the treasure hunters cloaked their operations in secrecy. It could be that treasure was found. If so, was it Blackbeard's—or was it Quelch's?

# 6. Mahé

*Seychelles, Indian Ocean*

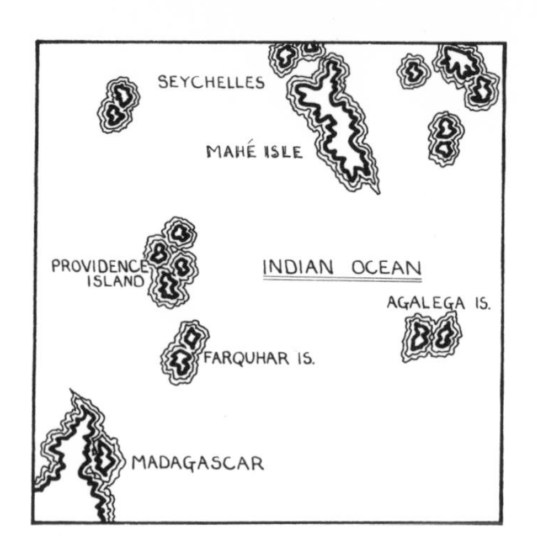


A French pirate known as The Buzzard was about to be hanged for his crimes. Just as the noose was adjusted around his throat he produced a roll of parchment from his velvet jacket and flung it to the gawping crowd, crying, 'Find my treasure who can!'

The roll of parchment was found to contain more than a treasure-map: it contained a series of clues to a lengthy and astonishing puzzle, based on the twelve Labours of Hercules and the achievements of Perseus (these are explained at the end of this chapter) which had to be solved before the whereabouts of the treasure would be revealed.

The clues were to lead to one of the most complicated treasure-hunts ever devised by a cunning and well-read mind, clues that would take the treasure-seekers to the idyllic island of Mahé, the largest island in the Seychelles. Solving the clues became a battle of wits between the little-known pirate and those who have vainly attempted to find his treasure for over two hundred years. One of the treasure-hunters actually died of disappointment when he thought he had finally found the treasure after thirty years of digging, only to find that the Buzzard had foiled him again.

The Buzzard had many names, as did most pirates behind which to hide their real identities. His real name was

Olivier le Vasseur, but he was known as Olivier la Bouche, or La Buse (The Buzzard) because he was one of the most successful of those pirates who preyed on shipping in the Indian Ocean early in the eighteenth century. The golden days of the Caribbean and South America were nearly over, and the new hunting-grounds for pirates were in the Indian Ocean as new trade routes developed between Europe and India, China and the East Indies.

The Buzzard had originally been given a ship by the

French government in 1715 and sent to the Spanish Main, in the Caribbean, as a privateer. When he was recalled by his government in 1720 he headed for France with his plunder, but on reaching the coast of South Africa, instead of continuing for home, where he would have to hand his treasure over, he sailed into the Indian Ocean and met up with two other jackals of the sea, Lieutenant John Taylor (formerly of the British Royal Navy) and an Irishman, Captain Edward England. With these three ganging together, merchant ships in the Indian Ocean had a very hard time.

The Buzzard scoured the sea for any ships carrying cargo. He kept the treasure but sold other goods, such as rice, silk, tea and spices, to the Dutch on the Laccadive Islands where the three pirates spent their shore leave and refitted their ships. According to all reports their main amusement on these islands was rape and murder, and the inhabitants were always very glad when they put out to sea again.

The three pirates were off the coast of Madagascar in April 1721 when they had at their mercy one of the richest treasure-ships in the whole history of piracy. It was the Portuguese ship *Vierge du Cap* which put up little resistance. It had very nearly foundered in a heavy storm before the pirates attacked it, and it had lightened its load by throwing most of its seventy heavy guns overboard in order to survive. Normally, the pirates would not have been able to get within hailing distance of the ship but in its present unarmed state it was no match for them and they took it easily. They were astounded at their luck when they realized who, and what, was aboard.

The Archbishop of Goa, the Portuguese Viceroy, and the Conde de Ericeira were among the wealthy passengers returning home to Portugal with their entire fortunes. The ship was a floating treasure-house. There were bars of gold and silver, chests of gold coins, pearls from the Indies, casks of diamonds, silks, art treasures, and all the expensive trappings of the Archbishop.

The passengers were ransomed and held on the island of

Madagascar while the pirates shared out the treasure between them. There was enough to give each member of the crew five thousand golden guineas and forty-two diamonds after the pirate captains had taken their share. The Buzzard got the Archbishop's altar treasures as part of his share, and Lieutenant Taylor also kept the Portuguese ship which he renamed *Victory*.

The Buzzard then sailed for the Seychelles and Mahé where he hid his treasure in a cave. He added to this cache over the years until it was worth several vast fortunes. It was during this time that he constructed his most elaborate puzzles and series of underground clues leading back to where the treasure was finally hidden. He had eleven years in which to engineer the puzzle—and engineer is the only word that can describe its elaborate nature—the answer to which only he knew, before he was captured by the French after a bloody battle and taken in chains to the gallows where he was hanged on 17 July 1730. It was the end for him, but only the start of the mystery for treasure-hunters.

The treasure-hunter who spent most time poring over the puzzle was Reginald Cruise-Wilkins, who came to Mahé in 1948 on a holiday. He spent part of his holiday in a hotel not far from Bel Ombre, the beach where the Buzzard's treasure is hidden.

Cruise-Wilkins met an old Norwegian whaling-skipper who had retired to Bel Ombre with the Buzzard's map and its seemingly unsolvable clues in search of the treasure. During his investigations on the beach, he had found strange markings on the rocks: there were dogs, serpents, tortoises, people, but he could make nothing of them. He told Cruise-Wilkins that he had spent the best part of twenty years searching for the treasure. Once he thought he was getting somewhere when he unearthed a large wooden chest; all he found in it were the skeletons of men long dead. He said he was now too old to continue the search, and if Cruise-Wilkins wanted to try, he was welcome to the map.

After a year spent studying the clues, Cruise-Wilkins believed he had a lead on what they meant, so he went to raise the money for what he hoped would be a short search. In the event, he was to dig for twenty-seven years and then die at the moment he thought he had reached his goal.

The first dig revealed a staircase, roughly hewn from sandstone, some distance from the shore. The staircase led to a large underground chamber, and then upwards into a high rock dome that, through an opening, commanded a view of the sea approaches to the beach. There were carvings on the wall of the staircase of Andromeda chained to the rocks to be devoured by the sea monster from which she was rescued by Perseus. The first clue of the Buzzard's map was solved.

Then Cruise-Wilkins discovered that the treasure-site covered sixty acres stretching back inland, all honeycombed with man-made underground passages. The twelve 'Labours' were in different areas, each having a parallel on the beach at Bel Ombre. One clue indicated that Hercules had to kill the water-snake Hydra. Cruise-Wilkins discovered this to mean that he had to divert an underground stream before he could enter a cavern that lay beyond. He found that the stream had already been changed from its original course to conceal the cavern. Another clue indicated that the Golden Apples of the Hesperides had to be picked. These were represented by three round rocks, dangerously balanced, so that he was nearly killed when he moved one which unbalanced the others and made them fall.

Each clue had to be solved before the next step of the search could be embarked upon, and there were many traps. All the Labours of Hercules were discovered from the clues on the map. There was the scimitar of Perseus (the blade of a sword in the rock); spears growing from the dragon's teeth planted by Jason (upright rods in the floor of a cave); the payment to Charon for ferrying the dead across the Styx (an old coin hidden in a hollow by an underground stream). As Cruise-Wilkins took and solved each clue in turn he discovered that the clues extended beyond the twelve Labours. The position of the stars and the planets at various times of the year had to be considered, and there were many false clues leading to dangerous traps. Cruise-Wilkins said that the Buzzard must have had a remarkable mind and a great deal of engineering talent. In fact, there is a fascinating similarity between the work on the beach at Mahé and that on Oak Island (Chapter 15). It seems that very similar minds must have worked on both astonishing projects, and that whatever was hidden must have been very valuable indeed to make it worth guarding so well.

Eventually, Cruise-Wilkins thought he was nearing the end of his search. He had solved all the clues. He had even built a dam to hold the sea back at one place on the shore, for it seemed that the treasure-cave was actually below the waves and could be approached only in this way. But then it appeared that the Buzzard must have originally entered the cave from a different direction through an underground passage, which the pirate completely blocked to prevent anyone else entering in the same way. Finally in 1977 Cruise-Wilkins stood on the exposed sea-bed looking at a slab of rock which marked the entrance to the cave. His team raised it and he entered, convinced after nearly thirty years' hard work, that at last he was to lay his hands on the vast treasure of the Buzzard.

The cavern was empty. The shock was too great for Cruise-Wilkins. He died of a heart attack.

It is impossible that the treasure had already been found and removed, because all the clues would have been solved, and would have been seen to have been solved. It is more than likely that the whole series of clues was a practical joke on the part of the Buzzard, that the real mystery has yet to be solved, and that this will not happen until someone can read what was in the Buzzard's amazing mind. Until then the Buzzard's treasure, which includes his share of the enormously rich haul from the *Vierge du Cap* and gold, jewels and silver from the East en route to Europe, remains hidden on the island.

Hercules was an Ancient Greek hero who was possessed of superhuman strength and who, when he was a youth, was accosted by Virtue and Pleasure and asked to choose between them. Pleasure promised him all carnal delights, while Virtue promised him immortality. Hercules chose to marry Virtue, and bound himself to serve the King, Eurystheus, for twelve years. He was given twelve tasks of great difficulty and danger to perform:

1. To slay the Nemean lion.
2. To kill the Lernean hydra.
3. To catch and retain the Arcadian stag.
4. To destroy the Erymanthian boar.
5. To cleanse the stables of King Augeas.
6. To destroy the cannibal birds of the Lake Stymphalis.
7. To take captive the Cretan bull.
8. To catch the horses of the Thracian Diomedes.
9. To get possession of the girdle of Hippolyta, Queen of the Amazons.
10. To take captive the oxen of the monster Geryon.
11. To steal the apples of the Hesperides.
12. To bring up from the infernal regions the three-headed dog Cerberus.

Hercules performed all these tasks and after his death became a god and, according to legend, a constellation.

Perseus was also an Ancient Greek hero, son of the mightiest god, Zeus. Like Hercules, he had many impossible tasks set him, one of which was to cut off the head of Medusa, whose hair was made of snakes and whose gaze turned those who looked at her into stone. Andromeda was the most beautiful girl in the world and was captured by a sea-monster sent by Neptune and chained to a rock. Perseus married her after saving her, and she gave her name to a star.

# 7. Mauritius

*Mascarene Islands, Indian Ocean*

When a pirate has a nickname like 'The Loot' it is only to be expected that his reputation as a successful buccaneer must be very high and that his treasure must be vast.

This certainly seems to be the case of the eighteenth-century French pirate with the rather grand name of Bernadin Nagéon de L'Estang. He lived during the period when the English state-owned East India Company ruled the wealth of the East—the gold of India, the rubies of Burma and the silks and jade of China. During the previous century piracy was at its strongest in the West Indies and South America, but by the time Bernadin 'Butin' ('The Loot') came along the balance of power and wealth had shifted to the Pacific, east of Africa, and he was probably the last pirate of any importance to prey on this great wealth flooding back to Europe.

'The Loot' lived at the time of the Napoleonic Wars at the end of the eighteenth and the beginning of the nineteenth centuries. After many years spent as a pirate he suddenly decided to join the French navy and, as he put it, defend his country against the English. Before he did this he wrote three very important letters to his heirs, telling them where his treasure—all the riches he had stolen from the East India Company and the Spanish—lay buried on the island of Mauritius.

The first letter, dated 10 May 1800, was to his nephew, Justin Marius, and reads:

> 'My dear Justin, should death overcome me before we meet, a faithful friend will hand over to you my will and documents. I urge you to follow my instructions and carry out my last wishes and God will bless you.
>
> Get our influential friends to send you to the Indian Ocean and go to the spot on Mauritius [referred to by him as L'Ile de France; Mauritius is its English name] indicated in my will. Climb the eastward cliff; taking 25 or 30 paces east according to the documents, you will find there pirates' signs to help you trace out a circle, of which the stream is a few paces from the centre. *The treasure is there.*
>
> By a peculiar combination, the figures of the cryptogram yield the name Butin Nagéon at this point. I have lost many documents in a shipwreck; I have already removed several treasures; only four remain, buried in the same manner by the same pirates, which you will find by the key to the combinations and the other papers which you will receive at the same time.
>
> The second treasure on Mauritius lies to the north of the former, with similar markings. By tracing out a circle at this spot and following the instructions, you will come upon it as upon that of Rodriguez.'

'The Loot' did not explain who Rodriguez was and in fact it turns out not to be a man but an island off the coast of Mauritius where there are many caves. In recent years treasure-seekers have found the initials B.N. carved on the rocks in these caves, and have even discovered them on the island of Pemba, near Zanzibar—all within the area where 'The Loot' roamed and raided before his death.

'The Loot' did not survive his time in the French navy

and in due course his will and second letter arrived. His nephew, Justin, who had already been excited by the news of treasure in the first letter, read it avidly.

> 'I am departing to join the ranks in defence of my country. As I will most probably be killed, I am drawing up my will and give my nephew, Jean Marius Nagéon de L'Estang, officer in the reserve, to wit: my land bordering La Chaux stream at Grand-Port on Mauritius and the treasures rescued from the *Indus,* to wit: it foundered in a creek near Vacoas; I went upstream and deposited in a cave the valuables from the *Indus* and there marked B.N., my name. I have taken the precaution of making my writings difficult to read; I will explain everything to Justin if I meet him.'

'The Loot' had not met Justin again before his death, for he was fatally wounded in a sea-battle. Before his death he wrote a letter to Justin's father which tells in detail his adventures as a pirate. It is obvious that none of his family were aware of the trade he followed, but 'The Loot' was weak and dying and he wanted to tell them everything. This third and last letter tells a story of sea-battles, shipwreck and piracy. One can almost picture the dying man summoning up his last strength to write to his distant brother, and although brief the letter is vivid.

> 'My dearest brother, I have been ill since we took Tamatave, in spite of the care of my friend the Commandant. I am weak and the fear of death is upon me. I am speaking to you for the last time, dear Etienne, and impart to you my last wishes. When I am dead, Commandant Hamon will send on to you what little I now possess and have saved during my adventurous life as a sailor.
>
> You know, dear Etienne, that my life's dream has been to build up a fortune to restore the splendour of our house. With the good will the First Consul has shown me after a glorious feat of arms I should have managed to do

so. But, as God will not permit me to carry out this duty and I feel death approaching, swear to me, dear Etienne, to carry out my wishes.

In the course of my adventurous life before embarking on the *Apollo* I was a member of the pirate band which did so much damage to Spain and our enemies, the English. We made some fine captures together, but during our last fight with a large English frigate off the coast of Hindustan, our captain was wounded and on his death-bed confided to me his secrets and papers for finding the sizeable treasures buried in the Indian Ocean. After first making sure that I was a Freemason, he asked me to use them [the treasures] to arm pirate ships against the English. But I was weary of this wanderer's life and preferred to enrol as a Regular and wait until France was at peace to find these treasures and return home.

Swear to me that your elder son will realize my dream and use this fortune one day to restore our house. The Commandant will hand over to you the writings about these treasures. There are three. The one buried on my beloved Mauritius is sizeable. As stated in the writings, you will see: 3 iron casks and large jars full of minted doubloons and bullion worth thirty million and a casket crammed with diamonds from the Visapour and Golconda mines.'

There were notes with this letter that explained the various locations of these treasures in greater detail and which contain such weird cryptograms as: 'Take a pair of pigeons, turn over the two hearts, the head of a horse, a *Kor fil winshient* shield; take a spoon' etc. There are Masonic symbols and references to the 'Little Keys of Solomon'.

Because of the long-drawn-out war, and various other factors, 'The Loot's' nephew never did make the long journey to hunt for this treasure, and in time the letters and notes were hidden away and forgotten. When the family eventually rediscovered them, they made little sense, and hunts for the treasure have yielded nothing. Even today a

Swedish treasure-hunter, Esperance Becheral, is still searching. He has worked at his excavations for over fifteen years, his work made more difficult by the fact that the site, near La Chaux stream is flooded. But he has found several tortoise-shaped stones, which he thinks are 'The Loot's' markers, and a wall that could lead to underground vaults where he is convinced the treasure lies.

Treasure has been found in other areas of the island, but since the island was used by countless pirates it probably has nothing to do with Butin 'The Loot'.

On one estate on the island an old tree was felled some years ago and a marble plaque was found in the roots which said, 'Here it is that I have hidden my fortune. You have a tree. At six inches towards the interior and N.W. you will see a cannon-shot. From the shot walk directly N.W. Sixteen feet away you will find a small stone. The depth of this stone is equal to the entrance to my treasure. Walk thirty feet to the S.W. You will discover a copper plaque 6 feet below ground He who has this will sing for joy for many long hours.' It is signed Corron de Bragile.

These instructions were faithfully followed and the plaque was found—but it was covered with incomprehensible cryptic writing. The finders decided to take it to Europe to get it transcribed at the British Museum, but the ship in which they sailed foundered off the coast of Africa and although the passengers were saved all their possessions, including the plaque, were lost.

On another estate in the south-west of Mauritius there is an enormous stone, partly covered with Chinese lettering, and words which read:

'13,800 ounces of gold, silver fine
Here you'll find a concubine
I leave you, monsieur, to divine
Without claiming from you what is mine.'

Nobody has been able to establish what that means, although many have puzzled over it.

So the fact that treasure is buried on the island seems to be undisputed. What remains to be discovered is the site of the buried treasure—and whether the treasure was 'The Loot's' or any of the other pirates.

# 8. Balambangan

*Borneo, South China Sea*

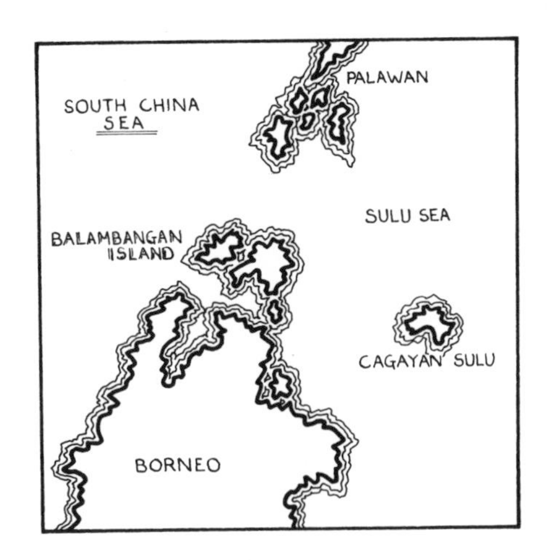


A few miles from the most northerly point of Borneo is an island so flat it hardly leaves the surface of the sea. It gives the suggestion of a sleeping crocodile. The island is Balambangan, and in Malay the word means 'not yet risen', referring to the wind.

These days the island supports barely half-a-dozen people who scrape a living there from the sandy soil and fish the way their stone-age ancestors must have done. It is a forsaken land, but once, for a few years, the mighty East India Company pinned its hopes on Balambangan and lost a million pounds there in gold coin, some of which, it is said, was hidden in a well and never recovered.

The mystery about the gold is traceable back to the year 1762 when a British fleet captured Manila from the Spanish and freed the Sultan of the Sulu Archipelago from their dungeons. Naturally the Sultan was grateful to his liberators, and to show his appreciation he gave the East India Company a part of the north coast of Borneo together with the island of Balambangan.

At the time, the Company had no need of either possession, though one of its officers urged the Court of Directors to occupy the island as a trading-post. He thought it well placed along the routes between China and Brunei, and it was in a central position between Japan, Korea, Bengal and the Dutch East Indies (now Java). Further, the island had two good harbours and sweet water and plenty of timber for building. The directors took their time in deciding and then sent an armed ship to secure their possession.

Eventually, the directors appointed a man called John Herbert as governor of Balambangan. Herbert sailed for Balambangan in the *Britannia* in 1770 and took two and a half years to arrive at the island instead of the estimated eight months, and in that time, due to some rather dubious trading activities, he had cost the Company some two hundred thousand pounds.

The *Britannia* dropped anchor at Balambangan on 12 December 1773, and Herbert lost no time in setting up a settlement and stockade. He had goods for trading, trained troops, British ships, a stockade to protect the settlement, and the goodwill of neighbouring princes. But it was not enough.

Herbert proved to be very active in drumming-up trade during the single year the settlement lasted. Money for the purchase of barter goods was spent in thousands of pounds. Expenses to the Company were high as well but, strangely, not one penny of profit was shown in the accounts. Money in the form of gold was massing on Balambangan, and it was destined solely for John Herbert and those few officers he trusted.

Herbert's first stroke of bad luck was by the time of his arrival the Sultan had died and the new Sultan of the Sulu Archipelago had no love for the English and envied them their power. He looked for a Spanish alliance that would rid him of his new neighbours and cancel the great debts he was beginning to run up with them over trading. That desire, Herbert's appallingly stupid treatment of the natives he himself encouraged to settle on the island, plus the fact that rumour leaked out that the island was a treasure-house of gold, sealed the settlement's fate.

Back in London, unease at Herbert's meandering journey to the East turned into amazement at the large amounts of money vanishing with no visible return. The Court of Directors sent off a letter of dismissal to their unruly servant. They were too late. By the time the letter arrived, Balambangan no longer existed for the Company.

Herbert's ill treatment of the natives did not confine itself to the peasants. To the ignorant Englishman they were all alike, peasant or prince. He put them all in the stocks when they incurred his displeasure—including the Sultan's cousin, Datu Tating who heard Herbert insult the Sultan himself. It was too much, and the Prince went off to a neighbouring island where, together with another cousin, he raised an armed band of three hundred natives.

The 4 March 1775 was Herbert's birthday and he wasn't going to let a few dire warnings upset his plans. There would be a big celebration, he said. It was pointed out that with the current unease in the natives' mood, and with the garrison reduced to a little over a hundred men, it was foolish to lower their guard. There were only two small brigs in the harbour; the larger ships were away trading. The settlement should have been on double guard; instead they were to enjoy a night of carousing.

Datu Tating knew about the settlement's weakness in troops and ships, in the weak defence of the settlement, and about the birthday party. He started bringing his men across to the island some days before the party, concealing them in the thick scrub.

By dawn on 5 March they were all in place, and by then most of the men of the settlement were blind drunk as they reeled to their beds after the party.

Reveille sounded as the night sentries marched back to their quarters, and then the natives attacked in three columns. Most of the British were drunk and without arms. The officers staggered around trying to rally the men, but they were too late. The attack had succeeded beyond Datu Tating's wildest dreams, and looting and burning began at

once. Governor Herbert escaped and made for the brig *Endeavour,* and watched in a fury as half a million pounds in goods and gold were carried off by Tating's men. It is surprising he did not counter-attack. When he took stock of the situation he discovered that he had lost only thirteen men, and that with some quick re-organization they could have fought off the natives instead of fleeing from them.

It is thought that Herbert was quite happy seeing the settlement and the falsified Company's books going up in smoke to hide his crimes. He is supposed to have hidden most of the gold he had embezzled down a well until he thought it safe to return for it and Datu Tating had not found this. In fact, however, the island was not re-occupied for twenty-five years. By that time nature had taken over, scrub had grown everywhere, and only the outlines of trenches, fallen walls, and broken pottery marked the site of the former settlement.

Herbert, a fugitive from justice, lived out his days in poverty and was never able to collect enough money to return to the island, and if he did stash his treasure of gold, amounting to millions of pounds, on the island, it is still there. No serious effort has ever been made to look for it. But if someone, sometime, cares to search the many wells on the island, now filled deep with the sand and debris of time, the chances are that he will come away richer than when he arrived.

# 9. Trinidad

*Brazil, South Atlantic Ocean*

So near and yet so far is an apt description of the vast buried treasure of Trinidad.

The story behind the treasure has all the ingredients to make it sound like exciting fiction, with its associations with Inca gold, revolution, pirates, and a map drawn on a tattered piece of sail. The story of the island itself on which the treasure is hidden is also incredible, with its mysteriously dead forests, wreck-strewn coast, and flesh-eating crabs.

In 1821, a young Spanish aristocrat of South American birth, Simon Bolívar, was sweeping towards the ancient Peruvian city of Lima with his revolutionary army. During the preceding seven or eight years Bolívar had freed much of South America from the centuries-old grip of its greedy Spanish masters, and he was now marching on Lima, stronghold of Spanish Peru. Stories of his battles during these wars of independence, stories of the killings and atrocities, had reached the rich Spanish families in Lima who decided to strip the city of all its treasures and flee back to the safety of Spain.

One of the richest buildings was the cathedral. Its interior radiated with gold, silver and jewels—the solid gold Virgin alone was twelve feet high—and all the other trappings of an enormously rich church. Much of the treasure was of Inca origin, and of incalculable antique value. All this, with ancient books, silks and paintings, was loaded on to carts by the panicking priests and wealthy families and, guarded by armed soldiers, the carts were trundled down to the harbour.

The soldiers returned to defend the city, and the treasure-ships, now manned only by their crews and a handful of priests, sailed out into the Pacific—and straight into the jaws of the waiting pirates of whom one was Benito de Soto. Living up to his terrible reputation as a merciless murderer and looter, he quickly slaughtered the crews, ran his sword through the wailing priests and civilians, and threw them all into the sea.

De Soto's immediate thought was to conceal the loot he had captured. Trinidad, rising wild and storm-swept from the tossing seas of the South Atlantic, came to his mind. Although far away, it was ideally located for his purpose. He knew of a cave there which he had discovered when taking on water during a slave-trading voyage.

The cave was at the head of a short valley between two towering mountains on the south-west bay of the island. One mountain was crumbling black lava and basalt, while the other was dark red. The lower slopes of both mountains were covered with brilliant green tree-ferns, and the cave itself, invisible behind a thick mass of ferns and vegetation, was marked by a rushing waterfall.

Landing the treasure was difficult and dangerous. Trinidad lies directly in the path of a prevailing wind of hurricane strength that blows in from the Andes, across the pampas—the great treeless plains of South America—and over the south Atlantic, whipping the island with huge waves. Added to this were the jagged rocks and high cliffs surrounding the island that made a landing almost impossible. Laden down with chests of gold and silver plate, de

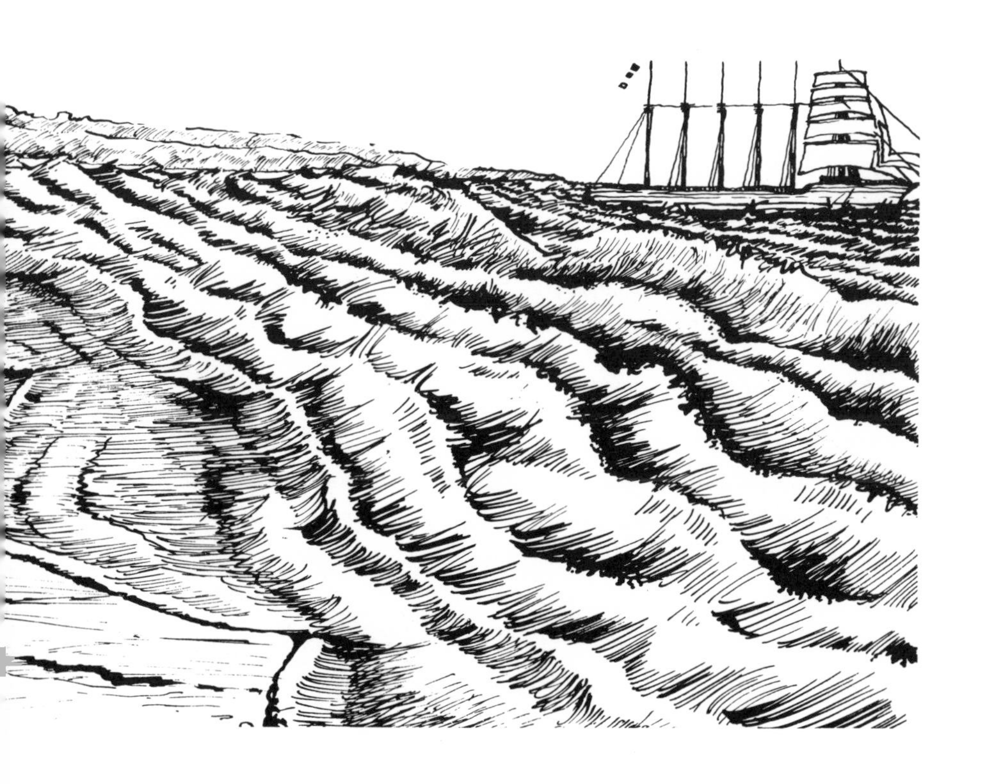

Soto directed the pirates as they struggled through mountainous seas and surf, along the valley and into the cave. The creepers and vines were then replaced to cover the entrance.

And that was the last anyone ever saw of the treasure.

Lord Dundonald, the feared and fanatical English naval captain and pirate-catcher, captured Benito de Soto and his crew on their way from the island, and took them to Cuba where they were tried and hanged. De Soto faced death bravely. Eyewitnesses reported that 'he walked firmly and erect at the tail of the cart bearing his coffin, holding a crucifix'. Were his thoughts on the far richer crucifixes hidden on the island of Trinidad?

The rope with which he was to be hanged had shrunk and stiffened in a storm that raged, so de Soto climbed on to his coffin, helped the executioner to adjust the noose, and cheerfully crying, *'Adios todos'*—'farewell all'—swung himself free of the cart.

His secret would have died with him but for the fact that one member of his crew disappeared from prison and so escaped execution. He was an educated and intelligent man, a good navigator, and was known ironically as 'The Pirate' by the crews of ships he later joined as a seaman, keeping quiet about his bloodthirsty past. They called him The Pirate because of the deep scar across his cheek, never guessing how close to the truth they really were.

After many years, The Pirate turned up as a quartermaster on a ship trading in opium in the China seas. The ship's captain was an Englishman, Captain Peters, who took a liking to The Pirate. When he was dying of dysentery in a Bombay hospital in 1850, The Pirate called for Captain Peters and confessed his whole story. Just before he died he told the Captain that in a secret compartment of his sea-chest was the map he had drawn on a scrap of canvas almost twenty-nine years before; it showed the location of the treasure on the island of Trinidad.

Captain Peters intended to explore the island on his return trip to England, but in the event he broke his arm as they neared the island and he could not leave his ship. He felt that he could not trust his crew with such a secret, so the opportunity was lost and, as it later turned out, this was the last opportunity for anyone to see the treasure again.

In 1888, Captain Peters persuaded a Newcastle shipping firm to take his son on a voyage to Brazil. They reached Trinidad during a particularly stormy period and for a week had to beat off the shore before being compelled to give up any attempt at landing. Having come so far to look for the treasure, young Peters decided to swim for it. The longboat was put out and went as close to the shore of the south-west bay as it dared when the foolhardy young man dived overboard and plunged into the furious breakers. The crew was convinced that he had drowned until they saw him through the white spume on the beach. They thought it would be impossible to get him off again, for the wind rose and the breakers increased their fury.

After an anxious night, the captain fired a life-line to the beach which Peters secured round his waist and, in danger of drowning, was pulled through the rough seas to the safety of the ship.

He had spent the night on the beach and had narrowly escaped being eaten alive by hordes of flesh-eating land crabs that swarmed everywhere so that there was no escape from their ferocious claws.

*The Times'* war-correspondent and sailor, Edward Knight, who spent more time on the island searching for the treasure than any one else, later described these crabs as 'saffron-coloured crustaceans who might well be the restless spirits of the pirates themselves, for they are indeed more ugly and evil and generally more diabolical-looking than the bloodiest pirate who ever lived. At night, the only resource was to rise and slaughter a large number of crabs when the others would devour their dead brethren, making a merry crackling noise all round.'

No wonder young Peters declared that nothing on earth would make him return. He reported that he had found the location of the treasure, but that a landslide of red debris from the mountain had completely covered the mouth of the cave, and that he did not think it could be uncovered without a great deal of hard work.

Seven years later another English party of treasure-hunters, in the *Aurora,* landed on the island, fully equipped with picks, shovels, timber and blasting powder, much of which they lost while attempting to land in the rough seas. They stayed on the island from 25 March to 17 April 1895, working either in sweltering tropical heat or in squalls and heavy winds, all the time being threatened by the 'tottering crags' that had the habit of falling and covering up their trench as fast as they dug it. They would have left much earlier, but their ship had sailed off to calmer seas. When it returned, the men signalled to be taken off. They were half-starved, suffering from exposure, and given to nightmares over the crabs.

Other treasure-hunters, mainly from America, had read about the proposed expedition of the *Aurora,* and had rushed to Trinidad hoping to get there first. The fact that none of them had a genuine treasure-chart did not deter them in their greed for riches. Many of them were unable to land, and of those who did nothing much is known. Certainly when the English ship arrived there was no sign of treasure-hunters, or of any diggings. Edward Knight reported that when he arrived in his own ship there was no sign of the diggings made by the crew of the *Aurora,* so frequent were the landslides and earth tremors. He had no doubt that soon after his own departure, all traces of his three months' work would be completely covered. He estimated that he and his team, working under very difficult conditions, must have moved about a thousand tons of boulders and debris from the head of the narrow valley, but many thousand tons more remained to be moved in order to expose the treasure-cave.

Unless there is another landslide that will miraculously sweep away all those thousands of tons of rock from the valley, it seems that Trinidad has made a good job of doing what Benito de Soto intended it to do—to carefully guard his now priceless treasure against all seekers after it.

# 10. Aruba

*Venezuela, Antilles Islands, Caribbean Sea*

North of Maracaibo and a few miles from Cape San Roman off the shores of Venezuela, South America, lies the little island of Aruba. It is practically impossible to reach the island except through a narrow and dangerous channel which leads into a bay flanked by a sheer hill of red sandstone. That blood-red hill and its many caves and passageways was the hiding-place of Domingo Mugnoz, an extraordinary man who wove a pattern of madness and the occult into his own life and into the lives of all who sailed with him under the skull and crossbones. The hill hid his gold and his treasures; it also hid his guilt as a defrocked priest turned murderous pirate; it hid his sexual fantasies and realities, his orgies and black masses, the dying cries of his horribly tortured victims.

This man's bizarre fantasies, indeed the very fact that he was a pirate, could all be laid at the door of an astonishingly beautiful blonde woman whom some called Wanda and some Rosita. Her name was most likely Wanda, since she was a Russian, but settling in Ecuador as she did Rosita came more easily to the Spanish tongue.

When Mugnoz was a timid and shy priest in Quito, the capital city of Ecuador, one who blushed at every woman, Rosita arrived with her new husband whom she had met and married during a trip to the United States. Rosita and her husband settled down on a hacienda near Quito, but Rosita quickly discovered that her husband was a drunken good-for-nothing who enjoyed beating her when he was drunk. Rosita retaliated by taking a succession of lovers, and fast and furious were the fights that raged between husband and wife and husband and lovers.

Mugnoz, to his great consternation, found himself listening to sexual perversions he didn't know existed when Rosita knelt in the confessional of his church twice a week confessing her sins down to the last detail. At first Mugnoz hardly knew what to say to absolve her, but as time passed he realized he was actually looking forward to her visits, and his little church soon became the longed-for meeting-place between himself and the woman he had grown to love. And the more he heard her sordid confessions the more passionately jealous he became.

It was 1820, and Ecuador was in the throes of a revolution against Spain. In the fighting and the burning of buildings, events became very confused, but what is clear is that somewhere along the line Rosita's drunken husband was found with his throat cut from ear to ear. Some stories say that Rosita did it and that stark naked she fled through the night to the priest for help, and that when he saw her in distress, he was so overcome that he threw his vows of celibacy to the wind and fled with her. Other stories, probably with more basis in fact, are to the effect that Mugnoz couldn't bear listening to Rosita's harrowing confessions any longer, and that with his black servant, he waylaid and murdered the husband himself.

Whatever the real truth, he and Rosita found themselves in prison accused of murder, and but for the revolution they would very likely have been executed. It seems that the chief of police guarded Rosita personally for her own safety, according to him, but before morning rebel forces invaded the town and released all prisoners from the town gaol.

Mugnoz, searching for Rosita, found the chief of police dead, lying in a pool of his own blood, and Rosita gone. He eventually traced her to the home of one of her former lovers and contrived her release by simply setting the house on fire and catching Rosita in his arms as she jumped out of a window. Pausing only to loot what belongings they could from the houses of fleeing Spanish families, the unholy couple disappeared and nothing more was heard of them until they reappeared off the coast of Venezuela, he, having lost all his former timidity and shyness, as a wicked pirate chief, and Rosita as his lady, at once recognizable by her flowing blonde hair, and for appearing on occasions wearing few or no clothes and adorned only with stolen jewels. Stories are told of how she stood laughing and beautiful and naked on the deck of the pirate ship as it went into action. Other stories describe her as being quite mad, chained naked to the mast by a golden chain.

An Englishman called Houston described how in 1825 when fishing in a small boat off the island of Margarita he was hailed by the captain of a pirate ship who wanted fish which, surprisingly, he was willing to pay for. Houston said the captain was a man with a pale face who spoke in a soft cultured voice, and at the helm was a sight that astounded him—a half-naked woman with long blonde hair chained to the deck and pulling at the chain like a captive animal.

They were a bizarre couple, certainly not 'great' pirates, but dangerous nonetheless, preying on merchantmen and slaughtering the crews. They even made the pages of *The Times* in London under the heading 'A terrible act of piracy'. The story was reported by Hugh Hamilton, a seaman on board *The Blessing,* which had been raided by Mugnoz and his twenty cut-throats. Hamilton reported how Mugnoz had made the captain of *The Blessing* walk the plank to his death under the eyes of his fourteen-year-old son and had then cast them all adrift in an open boat with no food or water. They were picked up on 18 July 1822.

Always after a raid, the pirates returned to Aruba, though they also had a hide-out on the northern coast of Cuba, where they vanished into the caves for an orgy of sacrifice, feasting, black mass and torture. Their favourite victims were captured Frenchmen, for Mugnoz never forgot the fact that Rosita was once kidnapped by her former French lover who had also taken to pirating the high seas in direct competition with Mugnoz.

Information about the terrible things that happened on the peak of the sandstone hill at Aruba was partly built up from rescued seamen and from one of Mugnoz's own men who had been captured. He described in great fear, since he was convinced that much of Mugnoz's power lay in the fact that he could make himself invisible, how prisoners were strung up over slow flames and roasted alive, and that Rosita would watch, dancing in front of them, and would finally stick a pike into their hearts. Then, on an altar laid out for black mass, the pirate crew would ravish her, watched by the anguished Mugnoz who, in a strange masochistic way, felt such punishment was his due to expiate his sins.

For the black masses and other ceremonies large quantities of beautiful and priceless jewellery were used from the accumulated stores of pirated treasure in their secret caves.

After four years Mugnoz, satiated with blood and destruction, left the sea to devote himself to black mass and to worshipping Rosita who by now seems to have regained her sanity and was no longer in chains. The crew were all given their share of the booty and dispersed to the mainland, but Mugnoz's black servant was recognized and was arrested by the local police, and after languishing for some time in a cell he was forced to tell the whole wretched story.

A massive raid was planned on Aruba. The police completely surrounded the red hill. In the network of caves they found the dying embers of a fire before an altar laid out with silver and gold goblets, a crucifix, and even fresh flowers, but of Mugnoz and Rosita there was no sign. They had completely vanished. Nor was there any trace of the proceeds of four years of piracy. No one but the two weird lovers knew where it was hidden, and they never returned for it. They were last seen in the forests of Paraguay by the local Indians who said they were both mad and naked.

And the piles of treasure, the jewels worn by Rosita and four years of stolen gold, still lie hidden somewhere on the island of Aruba waiting for someone to find it.

# 11. Grigan

*Philippines, Pacific Ocean*

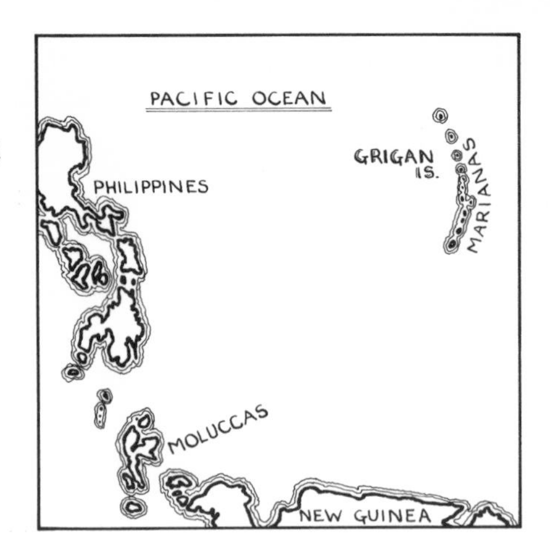


The enormous treasure of Grigan—two million gold coins—was stolen one hundred and fifty years ago for the love of a beautiful woman by an undisciplined Scottish mercenary. Because of his love, Robertson, the Scotsman, lied, cheated, stole and murdered in order to be wealthy enough to keep her, and it was because of her that the two million pieces of gold found their way to a tiny and haunted island in the middle of the Pacific, to be guarded by the ghosts of fifteen brutally murdered Tahitan beauties.

This story of blood, treachery and love began in 1820 during Peru's wars of independence against Spanish rule when Robertson, formerly a privateering sailor, was serving in the Peruvian navy as second-in-command of the brig, *Galvarino*.

Robertson was in search of a band of Spanish irregulars who were ravaging the province under their leader Benavides, a Spanish officer, and his second-in-command Martellin. Robertson landed his men at Arauco in Peru. During his search, Robertson captured one of Benavides' officers named Pacheco and, torturing him to the point of death, forced him to betray the whereabouts of Benevides' main camp. Surprisingly, considering Robertson's reputation for ill-treating prisoners, he did not kill Pacheco, and this act of mercy proved to be the biggest mistake of Robertson's life.

The Spanish camp was completely overrun and

Benavides and all his men, with the exception of Martellin who escaped, were killed or captured. Those who were captured were hanged, and Martellin swore he would seek out Robertson for revenge. Robertson, however, now decided that he had had enough of war and he retired to the small deserted island of Mocha off the coast of Peru, taking with him two women and a black servant.

Martellin, meanwhile, had become captain of a ship that quite by chance put in at Mocha during a storm. Robertson took to the hills but he was soon captured. Martellin intended to have his revenge on Robertson by taking him back to the same spot where Benavides and his men had been hanged, and hanging him there. Robertson, however, managed to escape from the ship just as an English man o'war was passing. He was hauled aboard the English ship and later put ashore at Peru where he joined the Peruvian navy—in pursuit of pirates!

His pirate-catching days ended when he found himself incarcerated by the Spanish in gaol. Robertson bribed his way out and headed for Lima where he fell in love with lovely Teresa Mendez. She had very decided views as to the type of man she would take as a lover. He would have to be (and in some cases had been) an aristocrat, an officer of state, an admiral—but only of the Peruvian navy—or the possessor of a great fortune. Robertson was none of these, but Teresa led him to hope that if he could win a fortune he would win her.

Robertson discovered there happened to be a fortune lying on his doorstep, or rather in the harbour—the *Peruvian,* which was laden with two million gold coins.

It didn't take Robertson long to recruit fifteen rogues and in the darkness of night they slipped out in a longboat to the unsuspecting treasure-ship, and in a very short time cut the throat of every man on board and set sail for the open sea.

An inspection of the ship confirmed that the gold was in fact there—a fortune. Teresa had filled Robertson's thoughts ever since he had first seen her, and now it looked as if his dream of possessing her would come true. He was not to know it then, but he would never see her again.

The fifteen men Robertson had gathered around him began to show early signs of discontent. They were under the impression that they would raid the *Peruvian,* collect their reward, and be back home by daybreak. And now Robertson was talking of taking the treasure to some god-forsaken island. To win them over, he promised them an easy life with wine, brandy, and food in abundance, and a beautiful woman for each man, in a balmy climate where life would be one long round of pleasure. They were convinced, and sailed for Tahiti to stock the ship with supplies. They had no problem in buying all the food and wine they needed, but it was a different story when it came to the beautiful girls they had been promised. They were such a disreputable-looking bunch of ruffians that the Tahiti girls wouldn't give them a second glance, so Robertson, in his inimitable way, organized another raiding party, this time on the homes of fifteen specially selected girls. The parents were knocked out, the girls were drugged and shanghaied, and when they woke up on board the *Peruvian* the ship was well on its way to Grigan in the Philippines. Most of the men were drunk and openly boastful of the kind of life that awaited the girls, and as if to give substance to their arrogant boasting raped several of the girls on the spot.

The more drunk the men became the easier it was for the girls, driven to desperate measures by the men's bestiality, to devise a plan for their own survival. They could not sail the ship so they had to defer their plan until they were on Grigan. When the men were stupified with food and drink, they set about stabbing each man through the heart. Nine of the men were dead before the alarm was raised. Robertson and the remaining six men stumbled to their feet and shot every one of the girls at point blank range.

The men hid the gold in a concealed cave, but they began to hate the island and could not sleep at night. They were convinced that Grigan was now haunted with the ghosts of the fifteen dead girls.

Another problem was the presence of the *Peruvian* in the bay. If they sank it, they would be marooned, and if they left it there it might one day be recognized by a passing ship, and the hue and cry would be on. Robertson's plan was that they take the ship to Manila and sell her, and return in a ship that would not attract attention. As soon as they were at sea, Robertson drew aside two of the men he felt he could trust, and put it to them that if there were only three of them to share the gold they would all receive more. He explained that they did not have to sell the *Peruvian* as he had enough money with him to buy another ship to get back to the island. As long as they kept it they were at risk. The two men agreed, and when they were within sight of the main Philippine island of Wahou, the four unsuspecting crew members were thrown into the hold and the hatches battened down. Then the ship was scuttled while Robertson and his accomplices pulled for the shore.

Robertson had no intention of sharing the treasure with anyone. He had been careful not to let any of the original fifteen men know the name of the island where they had concealed the treasure, nor its bearings, so the first night they were on land he took his two companions out drinking, and while they were engrossed in a game of dice he coolly slipped away and laid low for a few weeks with a ruined old sea captain called Thomson.

He persuaded Thomson, with promises of a share in the treasure, to charter a boat and crew to sail to Grigan Island, but when they were a few days out from land Robertson pushed Thomson overboard and assumed command of the ship himself.

That was the end of the matter as far as Robertson was concerned, but the old sea dog Thomson was an incredible swimmer and managed to stay afloat long enough to be picked up by a Spanish brig-o'-war. The brig was captained, by coincidence, by Benavides' former lieutenant Pacheco, the man Robertson had tortured at Arauco. From the information Thomson gave him, Pacheco set off in pursuit of Robertson, his zeal doubly strong, and caught him on the beach at Grigan. Robertson refused to tell them where the treasure was hidden, knowing that his life wouldn't be worth a candle once they had this information. His secret was the only thing that kept him alive.

Pacheco had Robertson taken in irons to the warship and strapped over a gun. Then with a cat-o'-nine tails soaked in sea water, he lashed him till the flesh peeled from his back. Robertson cried out for mercy and said he would lead them to the treasure, even though he knew that once

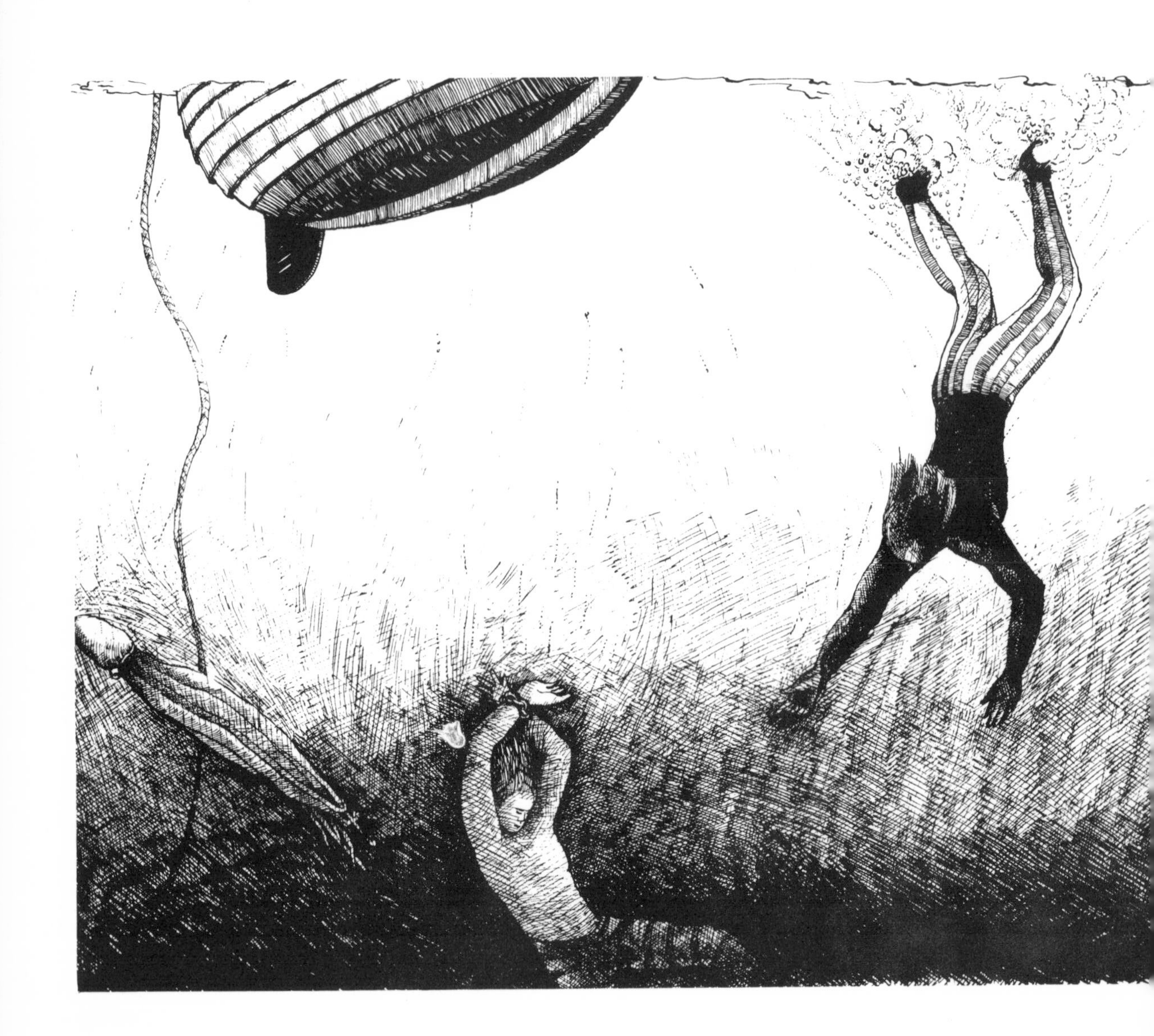

they had their hands on it they would have no further use for him and he would be a dead man. They took him in a longboat back to the shore, which was what he wanted. He was about to play his last ace. As soon as he was in the boat, he gave a sudden lurch sideways over the edge of the boat and sank, the heavy chains round his ankles pulling him down. A Spanish sailor dived in after him but Robertson fought with him and the sailor was forced to surface without him. When they did manage to get Robertson out, he was dead. It was his decision. If he could not have the treasure then no one else would. And to this day, no one else has found the treasure of two million gold coins—each one worth hundreds of pounds.

# 12. Taumatos

*Polynesia, south Pacific Ocean*

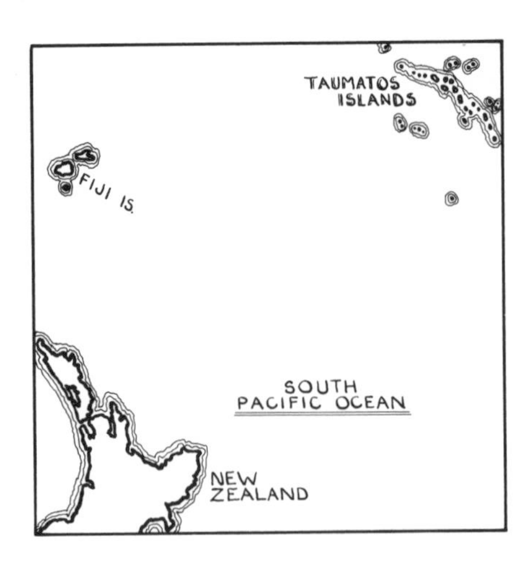


A little way up the beach of a coral island in the Pacific Ocean is a pear-shaped rock-pool said to be inhabited by deep-sea monsters. At the bottom of the pool are fourteen tons of treasure: seven chests of gold bars, each weighing thirty kilogrammes, several pairs of gold candlesticks, altar plates, silver goblets, and jewelled collars; and somewhere near the pool, buried in the sand, had been a small casket of jewels.

The island is Fakarava Atoll in the Taumatos group, which belongs to Tahiti. The church from where the treasure was stolen is in Pisco, a town on the coast of Peru in South America. It was stolen by a clever trick from the priests who had guarded it in an underground vault since the church was first built.

The gold was originally stolen from the Incas, the people of the ancient civilization which lived in the high Andes of South America and worshipped the sun. Much of the Inca's treasure was melted down for easy storage, and some was made into altar plate. Only a few pieces of the original works of art were kept. In the church at Pisco it was all put into an iron-barred vault that no thief could break into, and it was a well-kept secret until one priest, Father Matheo, ran away to sea to become a sailor. He told the story of the secret vault in the church to a rogue, Diego Alvarez, who in turn told three friends, Brown, Barnett, and Killorain.

Brown and Barnett were American adventurers; Alvarez was Spanish, and Killorain Irish. Both of the latter had once been good Catholics, and with that in mind the four of them worked out a plan they hoped would fool the priests. They relied to some extent on the fact that Peru and Chile were at war, and that in the confusion the priests wouldn't be able to think clearly.

Brown and Barnett went to Panama where they stole a small ship. When the ship was safely anchored in the harbour at Pisco, Alvarez and Killorain hurried to the church and, acting as sanctimoniously as they were able, poured into the ears of the priest in charge the story that the heretic Father Matheo with a band of cut-throats and Chilean soldiers was on his way to raid the church and loot the treasure. The priest listened. He thought no one knew about the treasure. The fact that these men knew about it, and about Father Matheo, convinced him of their honesty, and he proposed that they send to Lima, the capital, for help. There was no time for that, Alvarez explained; Matheo was on his way and would be there within a few hours. He suggested that the best course would be to take the treasure to the capital, where it would be safe. It so happened that he had a good boat in the harbour, and he would be more than pleased to place it at the service of the holy fathers.

The priest agreed with this plan and so the fourteen tons of priceless treasure were hauled aboard their ship. As soon as it was at sea the priests were murdered and their bodies thrown to the sharks. The four men congratulated themselves. It had been so simple. The next thing was to find a safe place to hide the gold—as far away from South America as possible.

They sailed to the Pacific and arrived at the Taumatos islands in December 1859. The island they chose was small and deserted with groves of palm trees and miles of white sand. There was a coral pinnacle on its eastern shore which made a good landmark to distinguish the atoll from the hundreds of others in the group. The chests were much too heavy to carry far up the beach and it was too great a task to dig holes big enough to hide them, so they sank them into a nearby rock-pool. The small casket of jewels which the priests had kept separate from the main treasure they buried in the sand for easy access when they returned later. Then the four men crossed to the neighbouring island of Nukatavake to ask the natives the local name of the atoll where they had left their treasure so that they could mark it on the sail-cloth chart Alvarez had drawn. But the island chief didn't like the look of them and was hostile. There was a brawl as tempers rose and an ugly situation turned into a fight in which the chief was killed, and so the men were deliberately given the wrong name of the island–they were told it was Pinaki.

The four men then set sail for Australia. They scuttled their ship off Cooktown and made for the shore in a long-boat, telling a garbled story of shipwreck to throw off their scent any would-be enquirers after them and their treasure. They went to the Palmer Goldfields. It was their intention to 'strike it rich', disappear, and then collect their treasure. They would then have an alibi to explain their great wealth. At the goldfields however they were involved in a riot, and in the fighting Alvarez and Barnett were killed; Brown and Killorain were sent to prison for twenty years. Brown subsequently died in prison. Killorain served his full time, and on release became a tramp, hoboing from place to place.

A man called Howe now enters the picture. Howe was a gold prospector in New Guinea in 1911 when he was speared in the back. The wound became badly infected and he made his way to Sydney for hospital treatment. During his convalescence he put up at a small boarding-house whose owner was in the habit of giving food scraps to a tramp who occasionally called at the back door. Howe met this man and described him: 'A wizened little ape of an

Irishman, about five feet three, with deep-set eyes and a thick shock of white hair. He was tattooed all over the arms and chest with the Union Jack, hands across the sea, naked women, and so on. He said his name was Killorain and that he was eighty-seven years old'.

Howe gave him several tots of rum and a few shillings now and again, and Killorain said that one day he would repay him. Howe then left Sydney for a few months and when he returned found that Killorain was in hospital and had been asking for him.

Killorain said he was dying. He told Howe about the treasure and showed him the faded map. Howe checked the Australian end of the story and found that four men had indeed been ship-wrecked off Cooktown in February 1860, as Killorain had said. The story seemed authentic enough, so Howe chartered a boat to take him to Pinaki where he arrived in February 1913, armed with picks and shovels and enough stores to last a year.

From time to time a ship called in at the island to see what he was up to, and what they saw astounded them. On a lonely, flat, waterless little coral reef they saw a man who alone had dug eleven quarter-mile long trenches, three to four feet deep, and at right-angles to all these trenches were others, making a criss-cross pattern over the entire island.

After seventeen years, Howe gave up and went to Tahiti. While there, he met an islander from Nukatavake who told him that if he had not been so secretive and aloof he would have learned that the island where he had spent so many fruitless years was not the island visited by the pirate ship. Alvarez and his crew had been misled because of their behaviour. The correct island was Fakarava Atoll, the one with the coral pinnacle on its eastern shore.

Howe went there immediately and at once saw the rock-pool. He dug at the spot nearby marked on the map and unearthed the casket of jewels which confirmed that somewhere in the inky depths of the rock-pool itself were seven chests of gold bars and other treasures. It was imposs-ible for him to raise it alone. Nor could he get help from

Tahiti as the French authorities would confiscate the lot. He took a handful of the jewels and dropped the rest of them in the casket into the pool for safe-keeping, and returned to Australia where he formed a consortium to recover the treasure from the pool.

And then Howe suddenly and mysteriously disappeared. Howe's partners in the consortium obtained permission to search for the treasure from the French owners of the Taumatos, and six of them sailed for the island. They located the rock-pool. It looked easy. First they probed the depths of the pool and at twelve feet hit a sandy bottom, but felt no chests. They probed deeper and through six feet of sand struck something hard. The diver of the party, George Hamilton, dived in and within moments was caught in the tentacles of a giant octopus. He fought it off with his knife and the pool was filled with the ink from the stab-wounds inflicted in its body. When he surfaced, Hamilton explained that the pool was tidal—it was connected to the sea by an underground channel.

On his second dive he was attacked by a huge moray eel, whose mouth is lined with jagged teeth that can tear a man to pieces. Again there was an underwater battle which he survived. But he would not go down again—the depths were too terrifying.

Empty-handed, the six adventurers returned to Tahiti where they purchased equipment to make a coffer dam—a square box they could lower into the pool inside which a man could work without being attacked. But the dam was not a success because they could not dig deeply enough into the sand without the hole filling up with more sand. They were forced to give up.

They went to London to raise more funds for better equipment. They advertised in *The Times* for contributors to join their consortium, and the next thing they knew was that they were all arrested for fraud. No one believed their story about looking for treasure.

George Hamilton wrote a book of his adventures (*The Treasure of the Taumatos,* London, 1938) which earned him a

great deal of money, and he decided that not all the gold in the world would take him back to the pool on the Taumatos with its horrific monsters—and its tons of gold.

# 13. Lord Howe Island

*Australia, south Pacific Ocean*

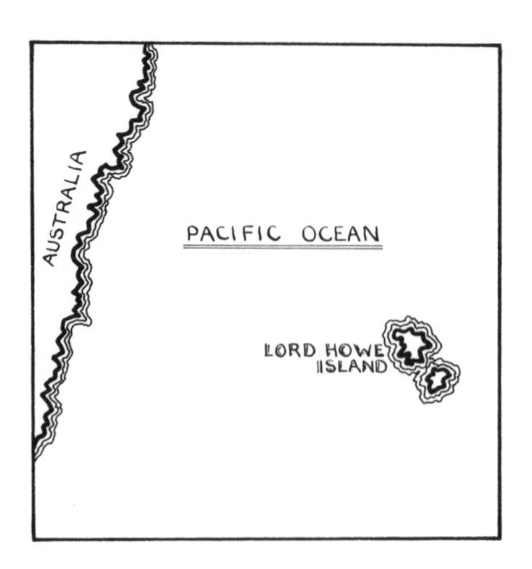


A mystery surrounds the golden treasure of Lord Howe Island because the ship in which it was carried should not have been there in the first place, and more important she should have been loaded with whale-meat and not with treasure.

*The George* was a whaler from Hobart, Tasmania, and in 1831 it sailed south to the rich whaling-grounds known as the Middle Banks, half way between Australia and New Zealand. She had a good voyage and did a brisk trade in whale-oil at Sydney and Hobart. After that, not too much is known about the official movements of the ship because her log was lost when she sank, but it later became clear, by information let slip by some members of the crew, and shipping records kept at various other ports (where *The George* should never have been, according to the sailing instructions from her owners) that the whaler and its crew were up to some very underhand business. Somewhere along her route she took on a cargo of gold and possibly opals from the rich Australian fields.

*The George* then sailed for Lord Howe Island to take on

water according to her captain's unconvincing explanation. There was a heavy mist on arrival, so the captain drew off for the mist to rise before sailing into the harbour where there were one or two rough shacks and where boats usually moored. The captain mistook his bearings, however, and struck a rock (now known as George Rock) and the ship began to sink. Seeing a deep bay in the cliff where the waterlogged ship had drifted, the captain beached her on the rocky shore, and before the ship broke up completely he and some of the crew removed their illegal cargo of treasure in the ship's boats to the shore.

Another mystery now arises. The island was uninhabited and was rich in fruit and game, yet the crew remained quietly in the area of the bay where they had been wrecked instead of making for the harbour where they would have been seen by passing ships and rescued. They stayed in their isolated bay for several weeks, obviously maintaining a cloak of secrecy. To do what?

Lord Howe Island had been first discovered accidentally in 1788 by a young British naval officer who named it after the First Sea Lord of the Admiralty, Lord Howe. Although attempts had been made to settle on the island, it was uninhabited when *The George* was shipwrecked on it. Eventually, though, the wreck was spotted by a merchant ship and the captain and only four of his crew taken off. Nothing was said then about other members of the crew. Later a whaler picked up the balance of the crew, but in a strange conspiracy of silence no explanation was given as to why all the crew was not taken off at the same time, nor was any mention made of any treasure.

Ten months after these strange events another whaler, *The Caroline,* sailed for Lord Howe Island. Her captain had not been involved in the original story, and had nothing to do with *The George,* but he wrote in his log: 'My mate said he knew where the treasure was buried. We landed in two quarter boats. It took us seven hours to reach the shore where we found a great number of bronze-wing pigeons. We shot seventy of them, but were unable to find the treasure as the country seemed to have altered considerably, my mate said.'

What seems to have been the case, according to the captain of *The Caroline,* was that his mate—who had been the captain of *The George,* and unable to get another berth as a master—did not recognize where the treasure had been buried. Rocky landscapes are notorious in that all landmarks look the same. He certainly seemed to have been confident that no other member of his former crew could have been there before him and lifted the treasure.

Over the course of the following years other attempts were made in great secrecy to locate the treasure, probably by other members of the crew of *The George,* or possibly by her captain of whom nothing further was ever heard after his brief appearance on *The Caroline.*

So the mystery of Lord Howe Island remains. What was buried there in such secrecy that the men dared not reveal their presence until their treasure was concealed? Why did it take them so long to hide it? Was it gold, or was it opals and pearls as has been suggested? And where did it come from in the first place?

The island is close to the biggest city in Australia, but very few of its people have ever heard of it, or of its treasure and the many unanswered questions that surround it.

# 14. Plum Island

*Nova Scotia, Atlantic Ocean*

In about 1870 there arrived in Shad Bay, Halifax, Nova Scotia, a tall stranger who immediately attracted a great deal of attention. He was described as being very muscular and handsome, greying a little at the temples, but with keen, dark eyes, and, to the entertainment of the locals, he was wearing a sweeping ten-gallon hat that lent him his nickname. Texas Allen they called him, and he did indeed come from Texas—although he said his name was Captain Allen. To begin with he was a little mysterious about his mission, but he soon began to talk—and, having started, spun a most unusual story.

In the early part of the eighteenth century a pirate captain, Edward Sweed, buried two small barrels full of gold coin, together with two hogsheads of Portugal wine and a tierce of old Bordeaux brandy on a deserted island in Mahone Bay—the very bay on which the small town of Shad Bay was situated. The pirates were later captured and, after a trial in London, were hanged at Execution Dock, in Wapping, where all the most notorious pirates met their end when caught. Sweed's wife, Sarah, visited him in prison and he gave her a map and other papers relating to his treasure cache. Sarah Sweed was an ancestor of Texas Allen's. He said that the papers had been in his family ever since, but there had been some doubt about the exact location of the island. When he said that it was called Plum Island, the locals shook their heads—there was no such island by that name in Mahone Bay, they said.

Texas Allen was very downcast, insisting that the Bay could be none other, and that all he wanted was to find the gold, over which so much blood had been shed. He piously added that he now wanted to use it for the good of humanity, though no doubt the people of Shad Bay took that with the pinch of salt it deserved. What Texas Allen didn't know was that Plum Island had another name; in fact, it had several, all names taken after people who had lived there, and it was right in the Bay where he could see it every time he turned his head. Some people called the island Corkran, or Cochranes's Island, and others referred to it as Redmond's Island. Small wonder, then, that the stranger from Texas was so confused.

Eventually, though, after several weeks someone took pity on him and casually pointed out Cochrane's Island—but, though he had a map, Texas Allen wasn't at all convinced, and he was to spend four years in Mahone Bay looking for a Plum Island that didn't exist. Finally, he gave up and left, but before doing so he gave all his information to Captain Pickles of Mahone Bay. However, there is some doubt about the fate of his treasure map; certainly Pickles didn't appear to have one, unless he was being devious, as all those Mahone Bay men seemed to be.

Pickles recorded that Texas Allen said to him: 'Captain Pickles, what you must do is look for an island with three mounds of rock making a triangle. The island is a small one, and at the head of a bay, and a little stream flows out of it at one end. On the eastern side of the rock triangle is a wall, not made with properly bonded stone or brick—but a dry wall, made by Englishmen in the old style. Close by the wall is a well of water, near a green and wooded gully, and in the well is the final clue to the exact location of the treasure.'

In the spring of 1872, so history records, but making it at least two years too early to fit the given facts, and soon after the departure of Texas Allen, Captain Pickles and William Baker—known as 'The Fox'—started looking for Plum Island. They sailed past one of the most famous treasure islands of all—Oak Island—and beat up for Shad Bay, looking for three mounds of rock that fell into the shape of a triangle. As they were eating lunch in a sandy cove, Pickles started idly drawing a plan of the island, as described by Texas Allen, in the sand with a stick.

The Fox glanced at the rough sketch and sat up. Pickles had drawn Cochrane Island—the very one that Texas Allen had been told to look at, but which advice he ignored. Pickles made such a noise, whooping and yelling, when the truth dawned on him that the sound carried to the devious Shad Bay men who watched the whole procedure through eyeglasses. They watched as Pickles and The Fox landed on Plum Island, searched for, and discovered, a cairn of stones, which they started to rip down to even more cries of glee.

The Plum Islanders turned up in force at this point, and one of them, Peter Coolen, stated that he was the owner of Plum Island, and demanded to know what was going on. The story was repeated to him and in no time at all the whole party was busy searching for the dry stone wall and the well. After some time and having found nothing, Pickles sailed off—some say to search for Texas Allen.

Twenty years passed, and in 1894 Jim Coolen, son of Peter, told his brother-in-law, Thomas Ganter, about Captain Pickles and his odd story. They decided to row to Plum Island and this time hunted for the well on the north end of it. They fell by accident into a patch of green bog. They were alarmed until they realized that there was hard ground under their feet. They somehow cleared out the bog until they found that the floor or base was of solid oak, the resulting shallow well sounding remarkably like the money pit in Oak Island. By then it was too dark to continue working, so they returned to Shad Bay and excitedly related the whole story. They were advised to contact Pickles without delay—he had all the correct information even though the directions were wrong. The men declined, which proved a mistake. Pickles was alive then. By the time they eventually gave in, and went in search of him, he was dead. And with him went what little information he had.

A treasure-hunt began which was to last forty-three years and which was to obsess Ganter for the rest of his life. At the bottom of the old well he said he discovered the information that he was to strike north to a hillock where there was a trench made by 'diggers of a bygone age'. This in turn led to a clue or marker shaped like a triangle on the east side of the island. At the base of the marker triangle was indicated a well, supposedly used by Captain Sweed in 1778 to provide his men with drinking water when they were digging out a treasure-cave in the hill, at its summit, and not base as was originally supposed. Near the well was the site of a fireplace where Sweed cooked. Ganter discovered the well and the fireplace under two feet of earth. The treasure cave in the hill was never found, even though Ganter spent all his money, dug huge holes, and employed massive mining equipment in his search.

No one has looked for the treasure since that date, so somewhere on Plum Island all the buried riches of Captain Edward Sweed are waiting to be discovered.

# 15. Oak Island

*Nova Scotia, Atlantic Ocean*

Oak Island is the scene of a baffling mystery in the world of buried treasure and one which has defied solution after two centuries of effort.

It is an accepted fact that there is treasure on the tiny island off the coast of Nova Scotia, but the question is what is actually buried there and, more important, how can it be raised from the deep hole where it lies? The actual site is known; one can stand there in an area of devastation that resembles a bomb-site and see the pit that is said to contain millions of pounds' worth of gold in wooden chests. So far, nothing has ever come *out* of the pit, but a million pounds has been poured *into* it in attempts to recover the fortune it conceals.

The site, when it was first spotted by a teenage boy in 1795, seemed uncomplicated enough. Sixteen-year-old Daniel McInnes of Nova Scotia took his old canoe one day and paddled over to Oak Island to hunt for game. While scouting for deer, he noticed that an oak tree on a low hill had a sawn-off arm and that on the stump a ship's block and tackle was hanging. Directly below the tackle block was a depression about twelve feet in diameter. It was not stretching his imagination too far to recognize from these signs that something had recently been buried there, and that that something must be treasure. Stories of pirates preying on New England shipping, of strange lights flickering on lonely islands, of men digging in the dark, and of ghosts that haunted chests of bloody gold were common talk at the time. Oak Island itself was said to be haunted by the ghosts of fisherman killed by pirates, but that story did not bother Daniel McInnes nor his two friends Tony Vaughan and Jack Smith with whom he returned on the following day with spades, buckets and ropes.

They started digging and ten feet down hit what they thought was an oak chest but which turned out to be a platform of oak logs, with all the seams carefully sealed with ship's putty. They continued digging and at twenty feet hit a second oak platform, and at thirty feet a third platform. As they bucketed out the loose earth, they could see the marks made by pick axes in the flinty walls of the pit. At thirty feet, the boys were forced to give up, and they tried to get help from some adults. But no one would go to the island because of the ghosts of the fishermen.

When they were older, Daniel McInnes and Jack Smith settled on the island and lived by hunting and logging, but all the time trying to find someone who would join them in exploring the pit in greater detail. They found this person in 1804—a wealthy businessman, Dr Simeon Lynds—and the three of them formed a treasure-seeking company.

Using equipment for removing earth from the pit, they found oak platforms—the purpose of which they could not fathom—every ten feet to a depth of ninety feet. At that depth they uncovered layers of tropical coconut fibre, charcoal, ship's putty, and a stone cut with curious symbols which they later deciphered as probably meaning 'Forty feet below two million'. They hoped that these were indications that they were getting near the treasure. After digging a further eight feet, their crowbars struck a solid mass which they assumed was the treasure chest. At that stage they gave up digging for the day. When they returned next morning, the pit was flooded to a level of thirty feet from the top. Although they worked for hours bailing out, the level of water remained the same, and they assumed they had hit an underground spring, and they were forced to suspend their operations.

A year later they hired men to dig a parallel pit with the hopeful intention of tunnelling below the water which they expected to be sealed off from the treasure-chest, but the new shaft also filled with water and collapsed. Dr Lynds had lost too much money on the venture and he gave up. For years McInnes brooded about the pit until his death. Then in 1849 Tony Vaughan and Jack Smith got the backing of a syndicate to reopen the matter. They hired drilling equipment and sank a pod auger—an open-centred drill which sucks up material as it drills—and at ninety-eight feet, the depth reached before the flooding, they hit a spruce platform. Below this was an empty space, and then the drill threw up in the following order: four inches of oak, twenty-two inches of metal pieces, eight inches of oak, twenty-two inches of metal pieces, four inches of oak, six inches of spruce, and, below that, thick clay. The new syndicate was wildly excited by these discoveries after only one day's work, particularly as they found three pieces of gold chain included in the loose metal. They calculated that the drill had penetrated through two chests, one on top of the other, filled with gold and jewels, but despite their excitement they were still no closer to solving the problem of how to get at it. The pit remained obstinately full of water.

A year later, with more funds, they dug another pit parallel to the original to a depth of a hundred and ten feet. It filled with water, but this time a workman fell in and when rescued declared that the water was salt—a remarkable fact to discover after forty-six years. They then remarked that they had noticed that the level of water in the pits rose and fell with the tides. Tony Vaughan said that at low tide there was always what he had taken to be a spring outlet to the sea at Smith's Cove—some five hundred feet from the Money Pit. The beach was dug and examined, and they made the astonishing discovery that nearly the whole area was an enormous sponge-catchment area to trap the tides. Below the sand on the beach they found tons of coconut fibre and eel-grass on a primitive concrete floor, and it stretched one hundred and fifty-four feet across the beach, and the full depth between the high and low water marks. Further away they found five rock-walled box drains slanting from the sea towards the Money Pit. The whole drainage system was designed to bring sea water towards the pit—not to take it away—and was lined with loose rock to prevent its collapse. It was an ingenious and remarkable achievement for anyone to have designed and constructed this on an island so close to the mainland without being seen. There was no doubt at all that this was hand-made by a brilliant engineer. It seemed that when the diggers removed the final oak platform they released a trap which opened the floodgates and let the sea in.

The syndicate decided that the only thing to do was to build a dam across the beach to keep out the sea, but being short of money they had to make do with timber, and this soon collapsed. They again tried tunnelling under the Money Pit to a depth of one hundred and eighteen feet, but this was no more successful than the previous attempts.

Expedition after expedition followed, all sinking their money into the Money Pit. By 1893 a newcomer, Frederick Blair, got the gold-bug and he was to spend sixty years and all his money trying to unravel the mystery of the Money Pit. He found the inlet of the flood tunnel into the pit at a hundred and ten feet. He then dynamited the other end of the tunnels near Smith's Cove to block the tide, filled the pit with water to above sea level to test its outflow, and threw in red dye. If it came out of the cove he would know that he had not succeeded in blocking the drains. No dye came. He was jubilant. Work could now start on pumping out the pit and the treasure would be his. Then he made the horrifying discovery that although Smith's Cove was blocked, red dye was coming in three different places from the land on the opposite side of the island, three hundred feet from the Money Pit. The Pit was between *two* flood tunnels, but no one has been able to locate the second, even today.

Blair then used an auger drill again. At one hundred and fifty-three feet it went through seven inches of ancient cement, five of oak, thirty-two inches of metal pieces, more oak and more cement. At a hundred and seventy feet the drill could go no further. There was a layer of solid iron it was unable to pierce. This time the drill produced gold slurrings and a scrap of parchment bearing the letters 'vi' written in Indian ink with a quill pen, vital evidence concerning the age of the treasure. Blair thought that the layers of concrete formed an underground watertight chamber holding chests full of important documents.

The syndicate spent all its money and gave up, but Blair secured the treasure-trove rights to the island for forty years where he remained puzzling over its mystery.

Syndicate after syndicate leased rights from Blair, but all lost their money before retiring, defeated. They tried everything, from freezing the earth around the pit, digging

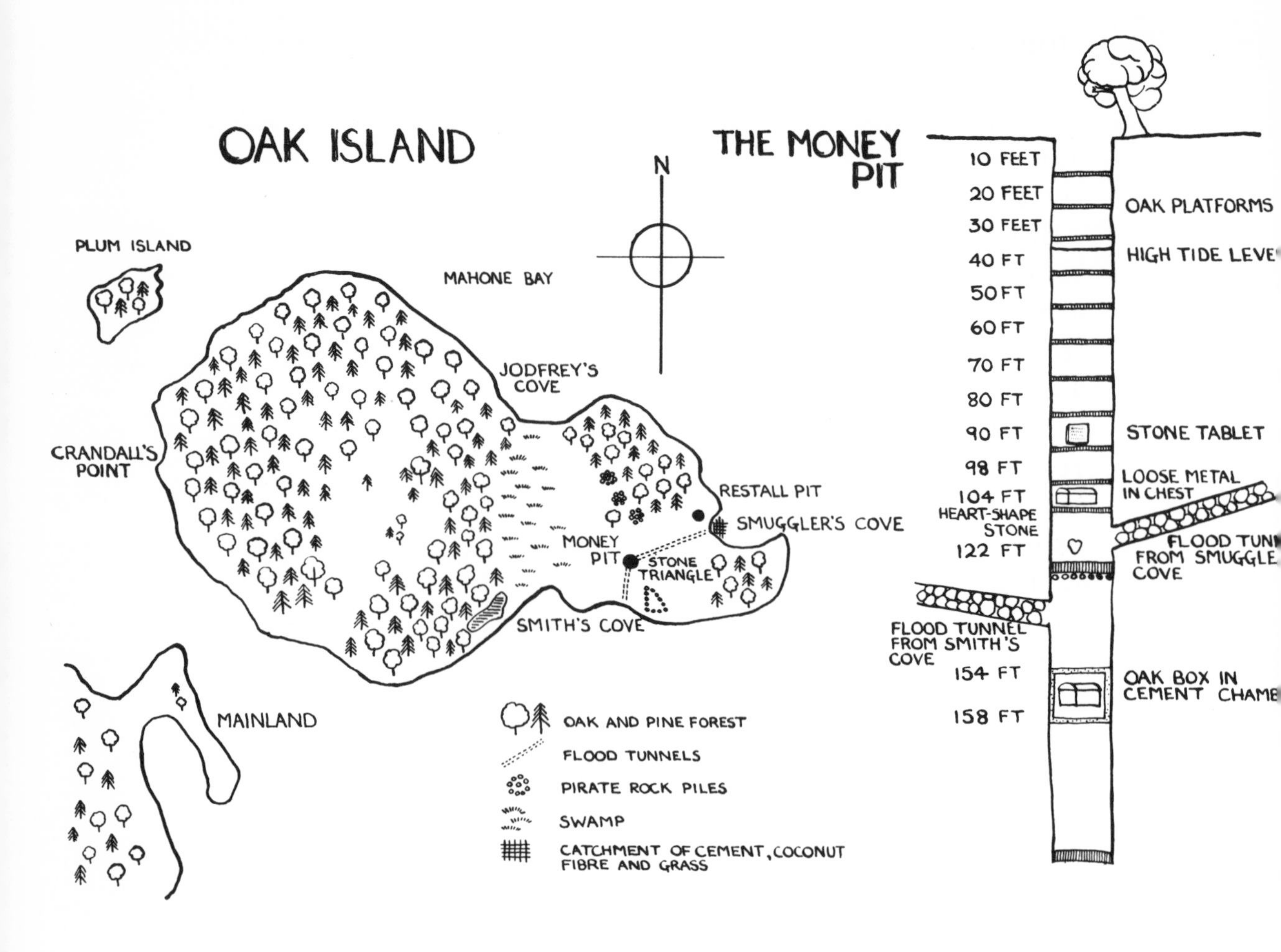


a moat around the pit and filling it with concrete, to steel coffer dams with divers—all without success.

After Blair's death, a Canadian, Bob Restall, moved to Oak Island with his wife and two children, and they have lived there ever since in a shack next to the bomb crater that the Money Pit now resembles, trying to work out how to get at whatever lies at the bottom of the pit.

In 1971 another discovery was made by treasure-hunters who managed to dig a narrow shaft to by-pass the flood tunnels to a depth of two hundred and thirty-five feet.

They found themselves in a huge cavern which extended *below* the Money Pit—so at least it is now known that the pit is no deeper than that. It had the appearance of being a 'solution cavern', that is, a cavern formed in limestone regions by the action of water (potholes are formed in this way). But what baffled the men was that the natural cavern was flooded by a man-made tunnel leading to the beach.

Some people think that the Money Pit was sunk as a blind to distract people from the real treasure which is concealed elsewhere. They say that the oak tree with the pulley and the sawn-off arm was too obvious. If someone went to the great trouble of building the flood tunnels, why would they leave the pulley? Indeed, a stone triangle was found in the bushes some distance from the Pit, with an arrow pointing due north of the Pit, but the significance of this was not known.

It is frustrating enough not to be able to get at the treasure without the added frustration of not knowing what it consists of. What it is and where it came from can only be guessed, but the most popular opinion is that it is the vast fortune, worth at least ten million pounds, of Captain William Kidd who ended his life being hanged on Execution Hill at Wapping, London, and that the treasure is that of the *Quedah Merchant,* the ship he captured that was filled with the riches of the Great Mogul, ruler of India. Captain Kidd's treasure map was later found in an old sea-chest belonging to him, but the island shown, while similar in shape to Oak Island, was not named. Captain Kidd did spend time in the waters of Nova Scotia. Against this theory is that the unnamed island on the map is shown as being in the China Seas.

Another theory about the treasure is that it is that of an unknown pirate from Europe—the name Mahonne Bay in which Oak Island lies does mean a type of low, fast sailing-ship much used by Mediterranean pirates. Some say it is the treasure of Caribbean pirates wrecked off the shores of Nova Scotia and Oak Island in winter gales, but that is most unlikely and does not explain where they would get the cement in such large quantities, or the palm fibre.

Another theory states that all the missing crown jewels of France's Louis XVI including those of Marie Antoinette, who were both guillotined during the French Revolution, were hidden here by Royalist engineers, and certainly, Royalist engineers were very advanced in their knowledge.

Whoever constructed the amazing Money Pit with its complicated flood tunnels leading from the sea, its drains drilled through solid rock, its 'sponge trap' for water on the shore, knew exactly what he was doing, and had years in which to do it.

One wonders why the engineers who have sent a rocket to the moon just don't go along to Oak Island and finally solve the mystery!

# 16. Caldy Island

*South Wales, Bristol Channel*

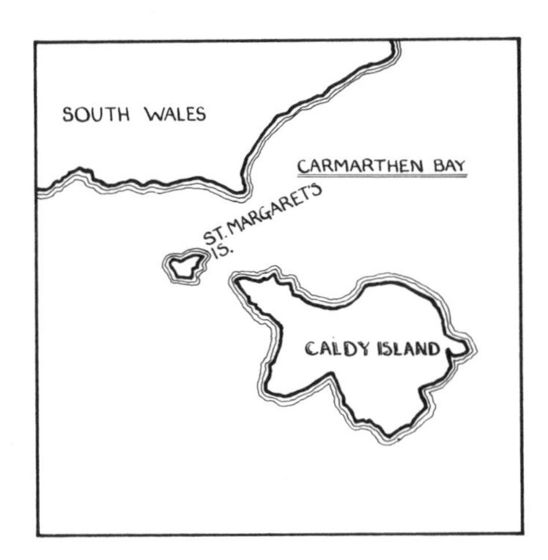


The small storm-tossed island of Caldy, which lies so close to the coast of south Wales, is said to hide the long-vanished treasures of Glastonbury Abbey in Somerset—including the Abbot's fabulous sapphire. But more, it could also be the hiding-place of the legendary Holy Grail.

To many people the Holy Grail is only a religious myth, the romantic object that King Arthur and the Knights of the Round Table searched for, a symbol of all that was pure. To others the Holy Grail is as factual as the Cross itself—although it has never, in fact, had any historical substance or form.

It is supposed to be the chalice from which Crhist drank during the Last Supper—and on which the Mass is based. It was said that Joseph of Arimathea, the first missionary to come to England, used it to catch His blood as He hung on the cross.

A less popular version of what the Holy Grail represents is that it was the shallow dish—a wooden platter—on which the bread of the Last Supper was broken and served.

King Arthur—whose magical city Camelot is supposed

to be in Somerset, not far from Glastonbury—always declared that the Holy Grail was a rare jewelled goblet, but this is most unlikely if it is indeed one of the objects used by Christ, who had nothing rich or exotic in His whole life. It is possible, of course, that the original wooden object was coated in pure gold later, as was done by some Catholic churches to holy relics. If it exists—and there is no reall reason to suppose that it does not; legend is frequently based on fact—and if it is made of wood and not of precious metal, the Grail would still be beyond price and unique.

The monks of Glastonbury Abbey never claimed to have had the Grail, nor did they claim that Joseph of Arimathea brought it with him when he arrived in Britain, although they did claim that he planted his staff at the site of the Abbey, and that it rooted and grew into the famous thorn tree.

However, it is strange that the legend stubbornly clings to Glastonbury. It was even said that the tombs of King Arthur and Queen Guinevere were found by King Henry II (reigned 1154-89) who re-buried them, together with the Grail, before the high altar in Glastonbury Abbey, thus linking the Grail with King Arthur and both with the Abbey.

Glastonbury Abbey was raided by Henry VIII's Royal Commissioners in 1534, during the dissolution of the monasteries. The abbot, Whyling, anticipated the raid and most of the Abbey's great treasures vanished. These included the fabulous sapphire, a pair of golden gates, many jewels, and the entire altar treasure plus, as legend has it, the Grail itself. There was also a vast quqntity of money—the Abbey was one of the richest in England—and some of this was found by the Commissioners, who were so angry that most of the wealth had escaped them that they tortured and executed the Abbot without a trial. He died without revealing the hiding-place of the bulk of the treasure, which has never been found to this day.

Why, then, should it be supposed that any of the treasure, and possibly the Holy Grail, made its way to Caldy? Such a question is astonishing, but there is a possibility that it could be on this small island off the south coast of Wales.

Glastonbury is in Somerset, a short journey from Bridgewater and then a dangerous sea-trip to the remote cliff-bound island, and any treasure would be safe there for a while, at least safer than it would be in England. Further, Benedictine monks owned the small abbey on Caldy, and Benedictines also owned Glastonbury. It seems very likely that Caldy would have been chosen as the treasure's hiding-place for that very reason.

Another story has it that Abbot Whyling sent the Holy Grail not to Caldy but to the dissolute Abbey of Strata Florida in Cardiganshire which was run by the Cistercians, a different order of monks, and when that abbey was also dissolved the Grail—a wooden cup in this case—came into the possession of the Nanteos family. It is certainly true that the owners of the ancient Welsh mansion of Nanteos believe that they hold a fragment of the Grail. They have long held a damaged part of a wooden vessel known locally as the 'Healing Cup of Tregaron', claimed to be part of the Grail itself. This story can probably be discounted; in those days the mighty Benedictines didn't think too highly of the degenerate Cistercians, and certainly would not have entrusted the treasure to them.

Caldy is known as the 'Island of Saints'. The first sight of it across the sea from Wales suggests a place of mystery and legend, shadowy and wraith-like, veiled in the morning sea mists. Even on a clear and sunny day when the air is rich with the scent of flowers, there is an aura that the island is steeped in the veil of dim ages, that it has a past of piracy, smuggling and ghosts. It is a place, only five hundred acres in extent, of peculiar and unique charm that leaves the visitor not with a feeling of sad hauntings but of happiness. Today the Abbey and the island belong to Cistercian Trappists, monks who make sweet wine and perfume, who till the land and grow their own food, and who refuse to discuss the treasure, or ghosts.

Some visitors say that Caldy has been haunted for a thousand years. There is the story, traced back in ancient writings to the sixth century, of Piro, the island's first abbot who forgot his faith so far that he fell into a drunken stupor and tumbled into a well, thought to be the abbey's lily-pool. He was fished out, but died that evening. His ghost is said to appear with the full moon during the grape harvest.

Another tale concerns the Black Monk whose ghost is thought to keep eternal vigil over the treasure of Glastonbury. It was his task, and his secret, known only to the abbot of Caldy at the time, to guard the treasure in its hiding-place. This was thought to be in a concealed room in a wall. When the abbot and the monk died, the secret of the treasure died with them. But the monk is said to guard it still, and has been seen roaming quietly in the grounds at night. Just before the Second World War a woman visitor was sleeping in a room once used as the monks' dormitory. She saw an apparition of a monk in black cowl. It crossed the far end of the former dormitory and vanished at a point in the wall where, as it turned out on closer examination, a doorway had once existed. The plaster that sealed in the door's space was covered with wallpaper, so the woman could not have known of the old doorway.

All trace has been lost of the records once kept on Caldy showing that the Glastonbury abbots sent a message to the abbot of Caldy of their intention to send to Caldy 'a portion of altar plate and divers other vessels, mostly of gold'. The Caldy monks don't admit to having seen any of it, but it could be that they are a little embarrassed by the rumour, supported by a photograph taken by a recent visitor of the ripped-out plaster in the old doorway seen by the woman already mentioned, that the sealed treasure-room was discovered and that the treasure was stolen by a monk. The legend of the Black Monk states that he is doomed to roam forever until the treasure is returned to Glastonbury—and if the treasure has been stolen, that will be a long time.

Caldy also has a history of piracy. The island's most famous pirate was John Paul Jones who scoured the Irish Sea and Bristol Channel for ships returning home from the West Indies laden with goods and treasure. He and his cut-

throat crew raided a ship, ransacked it, and then sank it with all hands aboard, so that none lived to accuse him. But he was too ambitious and became so obsessed with the acquisition of wealth that he failed to notice the murmurings of dissatisfaction among his crew. One night, while supervising the excavation of a hole in a cliff in Caldy in which to bury yet another shipload of treasure, he was murdered by his second-in-command and his body pushed into a cleft in the rocks, as if standing guard over the wealth he never lived to enjoy.

His ghost is rumoured to roam the cliffs and shores on moonlit nights. Certain psychic people claim to have seen him on the eve of All Souls 'surrounded by a number of his henchmen who carry an assortment of weapons equal to a month's output of Sheffield cutlery'.

There is no doubt that he and many other pirates used Caldy as a base from which to mount their acts of piracy, and a place on which to hide their spoils. The island was in an ideal position for them, guarding as it did the entrance to the Bristol Channel, the route of many merchantmen. In fact, things became so bad for the islanders that they had no choice but to use horses rather than oxen to plough their fields, since oxen were carried off as provisions in lightning raids by the pirates.

Many treasure-hunters have set sail from the shores of Britain looking for exotic treasure in far-away places while some of the richest treasure of all could well be concealed on a pretty little island just off the coast of Wales—treasure of immense value from Glastonbury Abbey, and unknown treasure of a different sort concealed by pirates.